From Flapping to Function:

From Flapping to Function:

A PARENT'S GUIDE TO AUTISM AND HAND SKILLS

● ● ●

Barbara A. Smith, M.S., OTR/L

ISBN-13: 9781533699077
ISBN-10: 1533699070

The author has made every effort to ensure the accuracy of the information herein. It is
the responsibility of the reader to evaluate the appropriateness of all suggested techniques
and materials included in this book. The author will not be liable for any losses, injuries,
or damages arising from its use.

Dedication

I DEDICATE THIS BOOK TO *my two sweethearts—my husband, George, and my son, David,—and to all the family, friends, and colleagues who have supported me along the occupational therapy and parenting journey. You know who you are.*

I also dedicate to Kreed Joshua, a young man who passed away on May 12, 2016. His infectious smile and loving family have been a huge inspiration for those of us in the autism community.

happy lives. You will not only find original activities to build hand skills (fine motor skills), but also learn how to look at your own environment and create activities that fit your lifestyle and individual needs.

From Flapping to Function was developed from Barbara's 30+ years of hands-on experience working with the challenges of autism and sensory processing disorder (SPD). Writing these experiences, activities, and wisdom down in a book is one of the most valuable assets a parent or professional can ask for. Thank you, Barbara, for sharing your professional knowledge and wisdom to address the multiple challenges of this very special population of individuals.

—Lois Jean Brady, MA, CCC-SLP,
Author of *Apps for Autism* and *Speech in Action*

● ● ●

This very clever book offers strategies and options, utilizing common household items, along with clear examples and photos of each.

—Marla Roth-Fisch, Award-winning author/illustrator of
Sensitive Sam and *Sensitive Sam Visits the Dentist*

● ● ●

Barbara Smith has written a practical, easy to read, how-to guide *From Flapping to Function: A Parent's Guide to Autism and Hand Skills.* The book provides an excellent overview and a logical progression of functional hand use. The point –form chapter summaries, DIY activities and clear illustrations are home and school friendly. Smith (AKA the Recycling OT) is a creative and original thinker and I thank her for writing this book with wide audience appeal. I am getting out my scissors now!!!

— Shirley Sutton, Canadian Occupational Therapist, and co-author of
Building Bridges Through Sensory Integration

● ● ●

Barbara has once again brought her professional knowledge and experience together to create a one-stop resource for parents. Just as her landmark book, *From Rattles to Writing*, proved to be a valuable guide to the development of hand skills, Barbara has organized *From Flapping to Function* to serve as an excellent companion tool for understanding sensory processing disorders and their impact on hand skill development. She includes important information about the link between functional vision, visual perception, and hand skills, as well as strategies for promoting handwriting. She provides teaching strategies that offer adaptations to assist with sensory modulation and continues her tradition for designing do-it-yourself activities that can be created from everyday household materials. I recommend this new resource has a place on your bookshelf!

—Katherine J. Collmer, M.Ed., OTR/L, author of *Handwriting Development Assessment and Remediation: A Practice Model for Occupational Therapists*

Handwritingwithkatherine.com

● ● ●

Contents

Foreword

● ● ●

PARENTS OF CHILDREN WITH AUTISM face a variety of challenges on a daily basis. Barbara Smith knows these challenges firsthand, and her personal experience and professional expertise resonate throughout this book. Barbara is the mother of a son with autism, and she is also an occupational therapist with more than 30 years of clinical experience, specializing in developmental disabilities. Barbara lectures and presents workshops for parents and professionals all over the United States. She has written numerous articles on occupational therapy and various child development topics. She is also the author of two online continuing education courses on the subjects of autism and adults with developmental disabilities. Her book *From Rattles to Writing: A Parent's Guide to Hand Skills* won the National Association of Parenting Publications Award in 2011. In addition to Barbara's contributions as an occupational therapist and author, she is a certified sensory integration and hippotherapy provider.

I am truly thankful that Barbara is sharing her knowledge and wisdom once again. *From Flapping to Function: A Parent's Guide to Autism and Hand Skills* is a valuable resource that includes ideas, techniques, and suggestions that parents can use to guide and support the development of children with autism. As Barbara explains in this book, many children with autism do not use their hands in a functional manner. Flapping the hands and lining up small items often replace natural fine motor experiences that are important for the development of hand skills. Not only does this valuable resource offer practical strategies to encourage children with autism to use their hands for functional tasks, it provides information and techniques to promote improved sensory processing, the development of visual skills, and much more.

Here is what you will learn from reading this book.

* How do I reinforce positive behavior?
* What is a strategy that I can use to get my child to make eye contact with others?
* How do I get my child to cross midline or use both hands together?
* What is a visual schedule?
* How do sensory processing challenges impact development?
* What are some effective strategies to promote writing skills?
* How can computer apps be used as teaching tools?

This amazing book is full of resources and practical solutions that you as a parent can implement to best support your child with autism. *From Flapping to Function: A Parent's Guide to Autism and Hand Skills"* is a must-have!

Anne H. Zachry, PhD, OTR/L
Author of *Retro Baby: Cut Back on All the Gear and Boost Your Baby's Development with over 100 Time-Tested Activities*

Acknowledgments

• • •

I WISH TO THANK MY many occupational therapy mentors—both the colleagues with whom I have worked, and the many authors and lecturers whose work has given me creative sparks. Much appreciation goes to the many therapists in the supportive world of therapy bloggers who have shared their expertise, and to the parents of children with special needs who have shared their struggles and joys on social media. I learn something new every day from these parents, many of whom have deeply touched my heart.

Special thanks to the parents who allowed me to share photographs of their children being their beautiful selves. I express sincere appreciation to Dr. Anne Zachry for being the first person to read this book, for "loving it," and for writing her thoughtful foreword. I thank the readers who generously took the time to write testimonials and my extremely patient editor, Kirsteen E. Anderson, whose expertise as a speech-language pathologist and parent helped me to keep my writing down-to-earth and parent-friendly.

Finally, I want to thank my family—many of whom are quirky but make life meaningful and packed with adventures. You know how much I love you!

Introduction

● ● ●

WHEN I HEAR THE WORD *autism* an image of four-year-old Gary pops into my mind:

> *Gary is lining up cars, end to end, while children around him make their cars roll, beep, and drive over paper roads. Gary doesn't seem to notice what they are doing, even as he crawls over another child's leg to reach the bucket of toys.*
>
> *Gary glances at a toy just long enough to reach for it before looking away. He sits with his knees bent and feet outside his hips, in a position called **W- sitting** because his legs form a "W" shape (see photo 1). While picking up cars with his left hand Gary shifts his weight to his right side. His wrist is loose and floppy. He grasps the cars with his fingertips, as though they were slimy fish he wanted to keep from touching his palms. When another child jostles the perfectly aligned cars, Gary grunts and, without missing a beat, adjusts them. Then he abandons his cars, stands up, and flaps his hands while walking around in circles.*

You may have imagined a similar child—a child who does not play with toys the way most children do- or whose hands flap more often than play. A multidisciplinary team observing Gary would all contribute important findings. An occupational therapist (OT) would note that his **eye-hand coordination** seems fairly normal, in that he uses his eyes to guide what his hands do. On the other hand, Gary does not look directly at objects, he avoids using his palms to grasp them, and he seems unaware when his body moves into a space occupied by another child. These are signs of a

1. This boy is playing in a W-sitting position.

sensory processing disorder (SPD), or difficulty receiving and responding appropriately to sensory information. A physical therapist (PT) would note **hypotonia** ("floppy" muscles) and poor **postural control,** because he leans on his hands to hold himself up. A speech-language pathologist (SLP) would note his lack of social awareness—he doesn't even protest when another child bumps his cars. He doesn't use toys functionally or vocalize while playing, like the other children who are making their pretend cars drive, crash and say "beep, beep." The way Gary doesn't look at other children and repetitively lines up his cars would draw a child psychologist's attention. Gary's preschool teacher would be concerned that he cannot name the colors of the cars or engage in pretend play, such as forming an imaginary steering wheel with his hands and pretending to drive.

As the team discusses their observations, the picture of Gary that emerges is typical of children on the autism spectrum. The way that Gary grasps, manipulates, and uses the cars while ignoring his peers demonstrates difficulties with

- Postural control: his body and hands seem to be floppy and weak.
- Visual skills: he avoids looking directly at the objects in his hands.
- Play skills: he lines up the cars rather than using them in pretend play.
- Communication and social skills: he does not imitate other children or share the play experience with them.
- **Sensory processing**: he has difficulty interpreting and responding to touch and other stimuli.

Challenges in all of these developmental areas contribute to Gary's difficulty using his hands, which is my particular interest as an occupational therapist. This book explains how atypical development affects the way children with an **autism spectrum disorder (ASD)** use their hands. It also offers intervention strategies aimed at helping children to experience success and be as independent as possible in performing everyday tasks such as dressing, cutting paper, or writing their names. I will explain how the ways children use their vision, think, process sensory information, and behave all influence their hand skill development specifically and their learning in general.

The technical term for *hand skills* is **fine motor skills,** because we use the small, or "fine" muscles of the hands when grasping and manipulating objects. Traditional examples of fine motor skills would be stringing small beads or stacking blocks. Effective hand use, however, requires much more than good motor control. In this book I take a comprehensive look at how children diagnosed with ASD typically use their hands, what challenges they face, and what strategies can help them reach their potential. I stress *"reach their potential,"* because there is currently no cure for autism or its associated challenges. There are, however, many effective and fun strategies that parents can implement.

Who This Book Is For

I wrote this book first and foremost for parents. When I worked in early intervention and Head Start programs I saw how family education enabled caregivers to practice OT skills throughout the young child's day and night, seven days a week, whether at home, in the community, or on vacation. Many of these strategies are easily integrated into everyday routines and can continue to be useful as the young child grows to adulthood.

As an example, four-year-old Abdul prefers to line up objects rather than drop them through a small opening into a container. Inserting objects is an early skill that develops the eye-hand coordination to use shape sorters or push coins into a piggy bank. Abdul was motivated to insert magnets into the can shown in photograph 2 when an electric toothbrush was placed inside.

Caution: Use larger objects if there is a choking risk. Magnets are dangerous if swallowed.

The toothbrush created vibration and motor sounds that interested Abdul and made him *want* to hold the container. He had to use both hands together—an important skill that will be discussed later—in order to separate the magnets. Pulling magnets apart is an enticing activity by itself, but inserting them into a vibrating container is irresistible. This is one of my oh-so-simple, yet oh-so-effective strategies to help children to build hand skills.

This activity is also suitable for older children or adults who are developmentally ready to learn insertion skills. Many of the strategies described in this book can help older individuals with cognitive and/or motor delays to develop hand skills typically mastered at a younger age. Whatever the individual's age, always make sure the materials are age appropriate and the person has the prerequisite skills to learn the task. For example, six-year-old Bonnie refused to touch gooey substances, such as paint or glue,

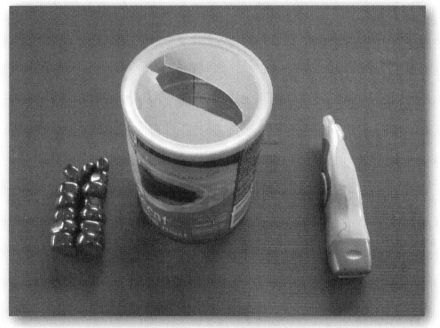

2. Placing a vibrating toothbrush inside a container
encourages Abdul to use his hands.

and she had difficulty learning how to form letters. Her mother filled a sturdy Ziploc bag with paint, and Bonnie imitated her mother using her index finger to form lines and shapes by pressing into the bag. Bonnie would not have been able to engage in this activity if she had not had the prerequisite skills to use her index finger as a writing tool, to visually attend, and to imitate her mother's movements. This activity motivated Bonnie because she didn't have to struggle with controlling a pencil, it was fun to feel the paint move through the plastic, and she felt like an artist without having to touch the gooey textures that she hated.

This is just one of many adaptations that may be beneficial to children who have sensory challenges, with or without an autism diagnosis. Many strategies may also help very young children who do not yet have a diagnosis but whose parents sense something may be different from typical development. Although children with ASD are usually not diagnosed until toddlerhood or older, some parents may notice developmental differences in their babies. Therefore, I include red flags and strategies relevant to babies. These may be especially important if the baby has older siblings diagnosed with ASD, because ASD is known to run in families. If the descriptions in this book "resonate" with your child, speak to your pediatrician or local child development center to get further information specific to your child's needs.

Much of the current literature on autism focuses on the social, communicative, and behavioral aspects of the disorder. I have written *From Flapping to Function: A Parent's Guide to Autism and Hand Skills* not only for parents but also for the early childhood professionals, educators, counselors, therapists, and other professionals working in school, residential, community, or institutional settings who seek a comprehensive resource that focuses on how developmental challenges may impact building hand skills and the strategies that will enable children to reach their potential.

Autism Spectrum Disorder Defined

The *Diagnostic and Statistical Manual* (DSM), published by the American Psychological Association, lists the formal diagnostic criteria for ASD. The criteria in the fourth edition (1994) were centered on three major areas of impairment:[1]

1. social interactions
2. communication, and
3. restricted, repetitive, and **stereotypical behaviors**

The fourth edition of the DSM listed five disorders under the umbrella term of **Pervasive Developmental Disorder (PDD).** These included autism and **Asperger's syndrome-**a term used to describe high-functioning individuals with autism.

The fifth edition of DSM (2013) combined the first two categories (social interactions and communication) into one and elaborated on the "restricted interests" category to yield the current diagnostic criteria:

1. social communication impairment, and
2. restricted interests/repetitive behaviors (including hyper- or hypo-reactivity to sensory input or unusual interests in sensory aspects of the environment)[2]

Note that the DSM-5 describes autism as a "spectrum" with varying degrees of severity, ranging from mild to severe. *Autism* now includes higher functioning individuals who would previously have been diagnosed with Asperger's syndrome.

Psychologists use the terms **hyper-** and **hypo-reactivity,** respectively, to describe atypically intense and diminished responses to sensory stimulation. Therapists and educators frequently use synonyms like *over-responsive* and *under-responsive*, and parents may describe their children as *seekers* or *avoiders*, or sometimes both at the same time. I will discuss these concepts further in chapter 2.

Gary, my imaginary child with ASD, lines up cars, a task that requires a high degree of visual attention and dexterity. In a 4-year-old child, lining up cars may signal a restricted interest or repetitive behavior, especially if other types of play are absent. On the other hand, many typically developing young children also enjoy lining up cars, so it's important to look for a cluster of red flags and not to panic over a single behavior that may be quirky but not atypical.

Although the DSM-5 diagnostic criteria do not cite difficulties with movement, motor signs are common and may show up differently, depending on each child's individual characteristics:

* subtype of autism
* age
* **cognitive abilities** (thinking skills)

* sensory processing—how the brain organizes and responds to information from the senses in order to learn

OTHER CONDITIONS THAT COMMONLY OCCUR WITH ASD

Autism spectrum disorders quite often appear together with other neurological conditions such as **attention deficit/hyperactivity disorder** (ADHD). However, these neurological conditions often occur independently of an ASD diagnosis, meaning many children who have ADHD or other diagnoses do not have the social and communication challenges associated with ASD.

Sensory processing disorder is also commonly associated with ASD. SPD is a controversial diagnosis because it is not defined in the DSM-5.[3] Yet many parents and therapists recognize that some children have unusual reactions to touch, sound, light, or movement—such as not reacting to a clap of thunder or running from the room when static comes on the TV. Children who have both ASD and symptoms of SPD often have difficulty attending to and tolerating certain types of sensations.

Other diagnoses that may cluster with ASD are these:

* hypotonia (low muscle tone, or "floppiness")
* **learning disability**—a specific condition that interferes with the ability to learn certain skills, independent of intelligence
* anxiety
* obsessive-compulsive disorder (OCD)—a type of anxiety in which the child repeats certain behaviors over and over
* depression

Intelligence is independent of autism. Children with autism may have cognitive abilities that range from severely below average to gifted. Diagnosis and treatment of disorders that commonly co-exist with ASD may help children better learn and develop functional hand skills.

OVERVIEW OF THIS BOOK

Part I of this book focuses on the challenges that impact building hand skills and the interventions to address those skills. Chapter 1 explains how individuals with ASD are unique, yet often share certain challenges in the areas of sensory processing, use of vision, mental processes, and behavioral differences that impact learning. Each chapter includes numerous creative and unique strategies that I have found to be effective over my 30-plus years of practice. Part II begins with a chapter that describes teaching strategies that promote overall hand skills, followed by chapters that discuss strategies specific to using apps as teaching tools, promoting handwriting, and teaching adults with ASD.

KEY TERMS AND CONCEPTS

If you are an educator, therapist, or parent who has been teaching a child with ASD for several years, you are probably familiar with much of the terminology and acronyms in this book. However, I wrote this book for readers who may not be familiar with educational and therapeutic jargon. I have already used acronyms ASD and SPD, and several more are to follow! Bolded terms are defined in the glossary, along with their acronyms, to help you learn this new language. Each chapter closes with a list of main ideas to review. In addition, the book closes with a "Do-It-Yourself" guide, resources, and endnotes.

ACRONYMS
ADHD: attention deficit/hyperactivity disorder
ASD: autism spectrum disorder
DSM: diagnostic and statistical manual
OCD: obsessive-compulsive disorder
OT: occupational therapist or occupational therapy
PDD: pervasive developmental disorder
PT: physical therapist

SLP: speech-language pathologist
SPD: sensory processing disorder

Summary: Introduction

I. Children with ASD may differ from typically developing children in their posture, visual skills, play, communication, and social skills, as well as how they respond to sensations.

II. Atypical development in these areas may hinder the development of hand skills.

III. The current diagnostic criteria for ASD highlight social communication challenges and restricted interests/repetitive behaviors.

IV. Some children on the autism spectrum may have secondary diagnoses of SPD, ADHD, anxiety, OCD, depression, or hypotonia.

V. Children may also have SPD, ADHD, or OCD without having ASD.

VI. Children on the autism spectrum may have below average, average, or above average intelligence.

Part I
Why Are Hand Activities Challenging for Children on the Autism Spectrum?

● ● ●

CHAPTER 1

Factors That Influence Hand Skills

● ● ●

BABIES FIRST INTERACT WITH THE world by wiggling their arms and legs with no apparent purpose other than enjoying movement. Over time, they learn to control their head and arm movements in order to look at toys and other objects, reach toward and grasp them, and eventually manipulate them using their fingers. Depending on their background, professionals may describe this skill progression as motor development, play, environmental stimulation, social interaction, or cognitive learning—and indeed, it is all these things at once.

Children with ASD tend to engage with objects and develop motor skills differently than typically developing children do. In this chapter, I describe the factors that impact motor development, play and learning, and how they often look different for children on the autism spectrum.

WHAT IS PLAY?

Nine-month-old Suzie sits on the kitchen floor, laughing at the sounds she makes by banging pots and pans. She is engaged, sitting with good postural control, manipulating objects, vocalizing, and sharing her joy with her father. But more than that, Suzie is PLAYING!

Suzie's play is fun, spontaneous, and deliberate. Nobody is telling her what to do, and she is not trying to accomplish anything. Suzie is simply enjoying banging the shiny objects together. She does not plan her actions, but she persists in them because she likes the sounds, sights, and feel of the pots and pans.

Play can be defined as "an activity freely entered into that is fun or enjoyable and that is appropriately matched to one's skill to represent an attainable challenge."[4] What constitutes an attainable challenge depends on the child's age and skill level: for a three-year-old it might be to scribble, but for an eight-year-old it might be to draw a self-portrait.

For babies and toddlers, play usually involves

- social, interactive exchanges with caregivers, such as "peek-a-boo"
- body play and movement, such as sucking on toes or clapping to music
- simple manipulation of toys and objects, such as shaking a rattle

A nine-month-old baby engages in simple manipulation play whereas a toddler uses objects with purpose—for example, bringing a real or toy phone to the ear. Suzie, the baby introduced earlier, might progress from banging pots and pans to pretending her finger is a spoon ladling some soup out of the pot in order to give her doll a taste. The latter activity involves both functional use of objects (mimicking the purpose for which the objects are used, such as cooking in a pot) and pretend play (such as imagining that her finger is a spoon). Compare Suzie to Gary, the child you met in the introduction. Gary's play is neither functional nor imaginary. Children on the autism spectrum typically continue to engage in simple manipulation play, such as lining up cars, after their peers have advanced to these higher levels:

- Functional play: driving toy cars into garages
- Pretend self-play: pretending to eat a pie made out of play dough
- Substitution play: opening and closing the index and middle fingers to mimic cutting with scissors

Studies indicate that children with ASD have specific play prefer-ences.⁵ They tend to be motivated by toys with sensory properties such as flashing lights or vibration. They prefer predictability, repetition, and familiar characters such as Thomas the Train or Sesame Street puppets. Some children seek out rough-and-tumble play that meets their sensory needs for movement and deep pressure, and many show a clear preference for or avoidance of messy substances such as mud or finger paint.

Each Person with Autism Is Unique

If you know a child on the autism spectrum, you may recognize many of the challenges Gary faced in the introduction. Although some individuals with ASD have excellent fine motor skills, many face challenges in this area. Every child is unique, but certain common characteristics impact the devel-opment of hand skills. Consider as one example Dr. Temple Grandin, an author, lecturer, professor of animal science, and arguably the best known individual with autism in the world. She has the intelligence and rare abil-ity to explain to some extent what living with autism is like. In her auto-biography, *Emergence: Labeled Autistic*, Grandin states that by six months of age, she no longer liked being cuddled and would stiffen when people touched her.⁶ As a very young child, she spent time spinning herself, flap-ping her arms, and drawing on walls. Over time, she learned that wearing tight clothing and lying under sofa cushions felt good. This makes sense because children with ASD and SPD usually crave deep pressure. In grade school, unlike many children with SPD, Grandin excelled in art activities using paint, paste, and cardboard. She loved carpentry and developed the dexterity to build a wooden boat model and sew costumes for school plays.

As a baby my own son, David, seemed to be developing typically, although he was difficult to soothe. At four months of age he and I took turns sticking our tongues out at each other, he smiled, he was visually attentive, and he loved to babble- all early interactive behaviors.

David's gross motor milestones were slightly on the late side—crawling at 8 months, walking at 16 months—but well within the normal range. **Gross motor skills** involve using large muscle groups, such as jumping with the legs or pushing a doll carriage with shoulders and arms. David preferred to sit in one spot for an exceptionally long time while playing, and he developed excellent eye-hand coordination and visual perceptual skills. **Visual perception** is the ability to make sense of the environment using vision; a common visual perceptual skill is putting together a puzzle. David could manipulate complex toys, and eventually learned to draw and construct them, using advanced visual perceptual skills similar to what Dr. Grandin describes having.

Unlike Dr. Grandin, my son spoke early, and I still love to brag about how at four years of age he announced that the force of acceleration acting on his swing was greater than the force of gravity pulling it down. David spent many happy hours at home playing with water and modeling clay. In kindergarten, he learned to calm himself by sifting sand when surrounded by screaming peers. As a Boy Scout my son could be found picking the blueberries that bordered the campsite while the other boys noisily packed for a hike. Today, as a young adult, he finds it calming to pick weeds and spread compost in the garden. Unlike many children on the autism spectrum, my son did not struggle with handwriting. In fact, David's excellent fine motor abilities continue to be a major strength and source of self-esteem.

Factors That Impact Hand Skills

Many children with ASD have difficulties with hand skills that cannot be explained by physical differences in their bodies, central nervous system disorders that affect the muscles- such as cerebral palsy, or profound sensory loss-such as blindness. Instead, children on the autism spectrum often have fine motor challenges because they develop atypically in the following areas:

* Sensory processing
* **Functional vision** and visual perception
* **Executive functioning**

Let me briefly explain each of these areas.

Sensory Processing Disorders (SPDs)

Children with SPD have difficulty interpreting sensations and using them to play and learn. They may react atypically to a stimulus such as a pat on the shoulder or a car horn as if it were intense or even painful. A baby with SPD might scream when placed on her belly, a toddler may refuse to touch wet foods, or a kindergartener may regularly break his pencils because he uses too much force. Although SPD impacts every area of a child's life—especially emotional, social, and communication skills, chapter 2 focuses on how it affects the development of hand skills.

Functional Vision

Children with ASD may avoid eye contact and look away from objects that they reach for. In addition, they sometimes have challenges with eye movements and visual perception that eventually affect learning to read and write. Vision is much more than seeing a sharp image. In chapter 3 you will learn strategies that promote functional vision—the effective use of **eyesight**—so that children can visually attend and coordinate eye movements to play and learn.

Executive Functioning

Executive functioning refers to how a person uses his or her cognitive abilities—the mental activities involved in thinking, understanding, learning, and using knowledge. **Cognitive ability** is related to intellectual ability, and the two terms are sometimes used interchangeably. Many psychologists and other professionals have been talking about executive functioning in recent years as they strive to understand why so many children struggle with sustained attention, organization, and time management.

Short attention span and distractibility are associated with both autism and ADHD. When I asked you to visualize a child with ASD, did you perhaps think of a girl who stops reading her book every time a car passes the house, or a boy who puts only one cup in the sink and forgets the rest of his dirty dishes when told to clean up after dinner? These are signs of executive functioning challenges.

STEREOTYPICAL BEHAVIORS AND USE OF SENSORY REINFORCERS

All children learn through repetition. For example, they might discover a movement or sound by accident—such as waving their hands around—then deliberately repeat it. Or they might imitate what people around them do—like clapping. Yet children with ASD take repetition to an extreme. They often engage in repetitive movements with their body (such as flapping their hands) or objects (such as shaking a toy shovel in front of their eyes) to the exclusion of skill-building movements (such as digging with the shovel). These repetitive movements are called stereotypies or "stimming," because experts believe the movement stimulates one or more of the senses. Stereotypies are not necessarily bad; they can be calming when children use them to meet their sensory needs. However, they can be a problem when they interfere with developing functional hand skills.

In chapter 5 I share strategies to decrease stereotypies and promote functional hand use through use of sensory stimulation and what I call **"sensory reinforcers"**—rewards that stimulate the senses and motivate children to repeat an action. For example, Beth hates to brush her teeth but enjoys putting an electric toothbrush in her mouth. The vibration provides the sensory stimulation that she craves. Because the vibration is meeting her sensory needs, she is willing to allow her mother to guide her hand to clean her teeth. When finished, Beth is rewarded with a big tight hug, another sensation she loves.

Life Skills/Functional Skills

Life skills, or **functional skills,** both refer to the everyday tasks we perform to take care of ourselves and be as independent as possible in our lives. Important life skills for children include hygiene, grooming, dressing, eating, play, and academic learning. An occupational therapy evaluation assesses how much support a child requires to perform both life skills- such as buying a school lunch and academic skills- such as aligning numbers in the correct columns to solve math problems. OTs evaluate the following developmental areas that impact abilities to perform both functional and academic skills:

Postural control, strength, and muscle tone, which influence how effectively children control their bodies while manipulating objects.

Refinement of grasps, such as using the thumb and index finger to pick up tiny beads, or using a three-fingered pencil grasp to draw.

Eye-hand coordination, using the eyes and hands together in order to catch a ball or touch icons on a computer screen.

Visual and visual perceptual skills, such as smoothly moving the eyes across a line of print or coloring inside the lines of a picture.

Tactile (touch) skills, such as tolerating the feel of an object in the hand and being able to identify what the object is without looking at it. Children with good tactile skills and body awareness are able to tie their shoes without looking at their hands.

Motor planning skills, sequencing a series of movements in order to perform a multi-step task such as pulling a shirt over the head or zipping a jacket.

Children with ASD often develop skills in these areas when engaged in activities that are meaningful to them. For example, Rhoda (see photo 3) has low muscle tone; she typically avoids using both hands together and

3. Rhoda is using both hands to squeeze a bottle.

looks away when using them. However, Rhoda is motivated to engage in the life skill of making chocolate milk. Squeezing the bottle of chocolate syrup provides sensory stimulation and helps her develop the skills of

- using both hands together
- gauging how much force to use
- tolerating touch to her palms
- visually attending and maintaining focus

⚸   coordinating eyes and hands to direct the chocolate into her drinking bottle

The hope is that Rhoda will be able to generalize, or transfer, the skills she learns from making chocolate milk to other functional and academic tasks, such as squeezing a glue bottle or using the right amount of force on a pencil to avoid ripping the paper.

SKILL GENERALIZATION

Typically developing children learn many hand skills through observation, imitation, and practice. They build on earlier learning to achieve more complex skills and are able to carry out the same skill in different situations. For example, Anne may first use large lacing boards, then generalize moving string in and out to use smaller ones or boards with a greater number of holes. One hopes she can then generalize the skills she learns through playing with lacing boards to, say, lacing shoes or threading a belt through belt loops.

Generalization means using a skill learned in one context—such as pressing a door opener button at Grandma's home to a new situation or environment—such as pressing elevator buttons in an office building. Most children easily generalize squeezing a bottle of chocolate syrup to squeezing bottles with various sizes, shapes, and contents. Many children with ASD, however, do not transfer skills so easily. They may need to be taught separately how to squeeze the shampoo bottle at bath time and the ketchup bottle at mealtime.

Let's look at a couple of scenarios that require generalization:

⚸   Brent was visiting his aunt Jean, who had bar soap instead of the liquid soap in a dispenser that he was used to using. Even after Aunt Jean wet his hands and lathered them with the bar soap Brent was unable to turn his hands over to rub both sides and then rinse as he did at home.

* Erma loved to help her mother bake and had learned how to spread butter on the baking dish using a piece of paper towel. When her mom realized there was no more butter, she showed Erma how to spread a layer of oil on the pan instead. Erma became upset because the oil glided quickly and did not require using the same force the butter did.

Children with ASD and other types of developmental disabilities often require structured training to generalize what they have learned to different situations. I will discuss this issue in detail in Part II, where I present a variety of teaching strategies.

SUMMARY: FACTORS THAT INFLUENCE HAND SKILLS

I. Play is an activity that is freely entered into. It is fun and spontaneous.

II. Typically developing children engage in play that becomes increasingly complex, beginning with functional play, then pretend play, and later substitution play.

III. Although children with ASD often have similar characteristics, each child is unique. Teaching strategies must be geared to each individual child.

IV. Using the hands efficiently to perform skills requires
   a. Sensory processing—tolerating touch and textures
   b. Vision—focusing on people and tasks
   c. Executive functioning—attending, organizing, and planning

V. Children with ASD often engage in stereotypies, or repetitive movements, that may be an attempt to meet their sensory needs.

VI. Sensory-based adaptations and rewards may help children to engage in functional hand skills instead of primarily stereotypies such as flapping hands.

VII. Occupational therapists typically assess developmental areas that impact learning both functional and academic skills.

VIII. Engaging in meaningful activities such as making chocolate milk helps children to develop hand skills to perform other functional and academic tasks.

IX. Many children with ASD may have difficulties generalizing what they have learned to a new situation or setting.

CHAPTER 2

How Sensory Processing Disorders Affect Hand Skills

● ● ●

A. What Is Sensory Processing Disorder?

CHILDREN ON THE AUTISM SPECTRUM frequently show a cluster of symptoms characteristic of a sensory processing disorder (SPD). SPD was formerly called *dysfunction in sensory integration,* and certain interventions for SPD continue to be called *sensory integration therapy.* The terms *sensory processing, sensory integration,* and *sensory organization* all refer to how the brain uses information from the senses in order to perform tasks as simple as placing a circle in a form board or as complex as orienting letters to the writing line. The brain interprets and responds to the following eight types of sensory information:

1. Visual: to interpret what one sees
2. Auditory: to interpret what one hears
3. Gustatory: to discriminate tastes
4. Olfactory: to discriminate smells
5. Tactile: to locate and interpret touch to the skin
6. **Proprioceptive:** to interpret where body parts are and how they are moving
7. **Vestibular:** to respond to changes in position and movement in order to balance
8. **Interoceptive:** to detect and respond to sensations originating within the body, such as hunger, blood pressure or urge to use the bathroom

During the first few months of life infants receive stimulation primarily through the tactile, proprioceptive, and vestibular senses as caregivers cuddle them, feed them, change their diapers, and soothe them with rhythmic rocking. These three senses are called the **sensory-motor triad** and sometimes described as the **near senses** because touch and movement sensations result from direct contact with the baby's body. In contrast, sensations from the *far senses*—sight, hearing, and smell—can be received from a distance as well as near the baby. The sensory-motor triad together with vision plays a critical role in developing gross and fine motor skills.

Children with SPD have difficulty interpreting what they see, hear, and feel, as well as how their bodies are moving. As a result they may appear to

- be clumsy when using objects such as wind-up toys or scissors
- not understand how much force to use: they may use so much force that they break toys or so little force that their shoe laces don't stay tied.
- either avoid or seek extreme sensory stimulation, especially movement
- struggle to tune out background sounds and sights in order to focus on complex tasks such as measuring with a ruler

Occupational therapists often create what is called a **sensory diet** to help children with SPD respond more effectively to what occurs in their environment. The sensory diet is like a recipe book of strategies adults can use all day long (and at night, too) to help the child accept everyday life events such as touching finger paint, sleeping through the night, or tolerating a haircut.

The sensory diet is individualized to each child. However, many children with ASD respond to deep pressure touch and movement by becoming calmer or more engaged in activities. An occupational therapist typically designs and monitors the sensory diet for a particular child, but parents, teachers, and others who spend time with the child may carry out the recommended strategies. In addition, parents often figure out early on how to meet their baby's sensory needs.

> *My son, David, was an extraordinarily fussy baby. I was surprised when a friend told me that most babies didn't cry **all** the time. She added that she didn't know how I could stand it. . . . Indeed, during his first year of his life my son cried constantly unless he was being nursed, rocked, patted on the back, or was sleeping. I think he cried in his dreams.*
>
> *Even though I had been an occupational therapist for two years prior to giving birth and had even worked in an early intervention program with many sensitive infants and toddlers, I didn't fully appreciate the value of movement and deep pressure touch until I become a mother. I read about how swaddling David and cuddling him close to my chest re-created the womb environment. He liked these things as well as rhythmic patting on his back. However, swaying seemed to best organize his nervous system—and it was the only sure strategy to stop the crying so that we could sleep.*

Fast-forward 25 years and I am working on a **hippotherapy** farm; *Hippo* is the Greek word for "horse." Hippotherapy is a specialty area that uses a horse's movement to achieve therapeutic objectives such as improving balance, coordination, and tolerance for touch.

> *Sitting astride a walking pony, four-year-old Rosanna bounces up and down as sensations travel through her arms. She hesitantly touches the mane—trying not to grasp it more than necessary. As 30 minutes tick by, Rosanna becomes more engaged, vocal, and willing to pat the pony. When I make the pony stop, Rosanna is annoyed. She looks at me, making eye contact for the first time that day. I show her how to point to indicate "go," and she imitates the gesture. I resume moving. In this situation movement functions as a sensory reinforcer, or reward.*

Neither my baby David nor my young client Rosanna responded to sensory stimuli the way typically developing children do. When given just the right type of sensory diet to meet their individual needs, however, David slept and Rosanna used her hands.

SUMMARY : A. WHAT IS SENSORY PROCESSING DISORDER?

I. SPD, formerly called *dysfunction in sensory integration*, refers to how the brain uses and responds to information from the eight senses.

II. The sensory-motor triad is made up of the tactile, proprioceptive, and vestibular senses. Along with vision, these senses play critical roles in developing hand skills.

III. Children with SPD have difficulty interpreting what they see, hear, and feel, as well as how their bodies are moving.

IV. Occupational therapists often create a *sensory diet* to help children with SPD respond more effectively to what occurs in their environment.

B. TYPES OF SENSORY PROCESSING DISORDERS

The impact of SPD can range from mild to severe. Most if not all children who have an ASD also show some degree of SPD. However, many children who have a SPD do not show the social and communication challenges associated with autism. Understanding SPD is complex because there are three primary diagnostic groups, and children often have more than one type. These three primary types are **sensory modulation disorders, sensory-based motor disorders,** and **sensory**

discrimination disorder. In addition, there are subtypes, resulting in a total of six recognized disorders.[7] I will outline the subtypes, then take each in turn, describing it in more detail and presenting suggested strategies for addressing it.

Sensory Modulation Disorders

    <u>Sensory over-responsivity:</u> These children are extra-sensitive to sensations, often picky eaters, and easily over-stimulated by sensations. They are sometimes called *hyper-reactive, over-reactive* or *avoiders.*

    <u>Sensory under-responsivity:</u> These children need a lot of stimulation to respond; for example, they can spin intensely without getting dizzy. They are sometimes called *hypo-responsive, under-reactive,* or *seekers.*

    <u>Sensory craving:</u> These children never seem to get enough stimulation; they are always moving, touching and chewing on everything. They may also be called *seekers.*

Sensory-Based Motor Disorders

* <u>Postural disorder:</u> These children show poor body awareness and low muscle tone; for example, they might slip out of a chair or lean their head on an arm while writing.
* <u>Dyspraxia:</u> These children have difficulty with motor control needed to perform tasks accurately (such as folding paper on a line).

Sensory Discrimination Disorders

* These children have difficulty interpreting sensations; for example, a child may keep stuffing more popcorn in her mouth, even though it is already full.

SUMMARY: B. TYPES OF SENSORY PROCESSING DISORDERS

 I. Most, if not all children with an ASD present with some degree of SPD.

 II. Many children who have SPD do not have an ASD.

 III. There are three primary types of SPDs.

 IV. There are the following six subtypes of SPD:

  1. sensory over-responsivity

  2. sensory under-responsivity

  3. sensory craving

  4. postural disorder

  5. dyspraxia

  6. sensory discrimination

C. THE IMPACT OF SENSORY MODULATION DISORDERS

Let's look more closely at the first primary type of SPD called *sensory modulation disorders.*

Sensory modulation disorders consist of

* <u>sensory over-responsivity</u>
* <u>sensory under-responsivity</u>
* <u>sensory craving</u>

Children with the sensory modulation type of SPD have difficulty with **self-regulation**. Self-regulation is the ability to control one's behavior, emotions, or thoughts and adapt to the demands of a situation. Children with a sensory modulation disorder may be impulsive, overly and easily stressed, difficult to soothe, or highly distractible. On the other extreme, they may seem lethargic, apathetic, or day-dreamy. Some children have behaviors associated with both seekers and avoiders! According to Tomchek and Smith,[8] most children with ASD have signs of sensory modulation disorders. Let's take a closer look at the three subtypes of sensory modulation disorders.

> Sensory over-responding, or super-sensitive: *Four-year-old George is easily overwhelmed by sounds, smells, movements, and things he sees, to the point where he frequently "shuts down" and cries. He hates to touch food, bubble bath, or fur, and often strips naked at home. George's favorite "toys" are rocks and blocks of wood, which he lines up in the basement. Repetitive body movements—such as rocking, flapping his arms, or flicking objects— seem to calm him. George will give familiar people a "high five"—but it had better be a firm one. His mom calls him "the Naked Curious Avoider."*
>
> Sensory under-responding: *Ten-year-old Dorothy frequently daydreams and slumps in her chair at school. She finds it easier to do her homework while bouncing on a ball chair, listening to erratic music, and chewing gum. Even with all this sensory stimulation, Dorothy's hand gets tired after writing a couple of sentences and she struggles to organize her sentences into a paragraph.*
>
> Sensory craving: *Twelve-year-old twins, James and Errol, are home-schooled. They both love to make funny sounds, stand on their heads, and have pillow fights. Their parents converted the basement into a small gym with a suspended swing, trampoline, and crash pad made out of pillows on a mattress. James and Errol follow a schedule that includes weight lifting, jogging, cooking—the spicier the better, according to the boys—making bread, and creating pottery between their academic lessons and weekly visits to volunteer at a farm. These boys never seem to get enough stimulation.*

Researchers have documented that sensory modulation disorders interfere with developing functional skills. Some of these children may have difficulty developing hand skills because they just don't sit still long enough to learn and then practice them. For other children it takes extra effort just to sit upright and still long enough to connect two pop-it beads or insert a straw into a juice box. Both sensory "seekers" and "avoiders" frequently have fine motor delays because they lack experience and practice in common childhood activities, such as building with construction toys or cutting out paper dolls.

Researchers disagree on which of the three types of sensory modulation disorders are most associated with ASD. In fact, many children appear to fluctuate between hypersensitivity and hyposensitivity.[9]

Sensory-based strategies aim to promote engagement and self-regulation and decrease **sensory defensiveness**.[10] *Sensory defensiveness* describes strong sensitivities to touch, movement, or other sensations. Children who have sensory defensiveness are often described as "avoiders" because they try to escape from sensations that seem neutral or pleasant to most people, such as a kiss on the cheek. To them, the sensation seems unpleasant, perhaps even painful!

Summary: C. The Impact of Sensory Modulation Disorders

   I. There are six subtypes of SPD, and children may have more than one type.

  II. ASD and SPD are separate conditions, but they often occur together.

III. Children with the type of SPD called sensory modulation disorder may be described as seekers, avoiders or cravers.

IV. Many children with ASD appear to fluctuate between being hyposensitive (under-sensitive) and hypersensitive (over-sensitive).

  V. Sensory-based strategies for children with sensory modulation disorders aim to promote engagement and self-regulation and decrease sensory defensiveness.

D. STRATEGIES FOR SENSORY MODULATION DISORDERS

Because every child is unique, it takes some trial and error to create a sensory diet that effectively promotes self-regulation. However, a good place to start is by exploring seating and positioning options, weighted materials, and fidget tools, which are described in this section.

SEATING AND POSITIONING OPTIONS

Many children—and not only those with ASD—focus and learn to use their hands best when allowed to move or find a more comfortable position than a chair. Some children may attend best when standing or walking! Movement, or even simply standing, may help children to learn because it sends more oxygen to the brain.

Positions that place the head in planes other than upright vary the type of sensory stimulation the brain receives. This is good for brain development! In fact, children who love to hang upside-down are giving themselves the sensory stimulation they crave and need. The boy in photo 4 seeks out activities that put his head in different planes while moving.

4. Moving with his head in different planes gives this
boy the sensory stimulation that he craves.

Changing head and body positions can help increase a child's engagement with hand activities. Explore these options to see which work best for your child:

5. Moving on a scooter board can offer vestibular stimulation.

* **Prone** (on the belly) with weight on the forearms or hands. While manipulating objects on the floor, a child can receive vestibular stimulation by moving on a scooter (see photo 5), a low bolster, or a swing.
* Cuddling inside a beanbag chair with heavy cushions placed over the lap or body can provide the deep pressure that helps children calm themselves and focus. A beloved dog draped over the child's body can help in the same way.
* A number of companies sell Bungee chairs. These chairs are made of strong cords that enable bouncing. Some children enjoy bouncing gently while engaged in hand activities such as popping bubbles or tossing beanbags at a target. Try alternating intense bouncing with slow bouncing during a hand activity.

- Sitting on a ball chair allows a child to bounce while working at a table or desk. Try wedging an exercise ball inside a box so that the child can enjoy gentle bounces without the ball rolling away.
- Seat discs, wedges, and cushions are other ways to allow a child to move while engaging in hand activities. For an inexpensive option, offer a slightly inflated beach ball or rolled-up sweater to sit on.
- Allow the child to kneel on the floor or a chair while working at a desk or table surface.
- Half-kneeling means standing on one leg while placing the other leg with bent knee on a chair or other support. Children can half-kneel while working at a desk or table.
- Turn a chair backwards so that the child straddles the seat facing the backrest (see photo 6). Children may like to wrap their legs around the chair legs or support their arms on the chair back while working.

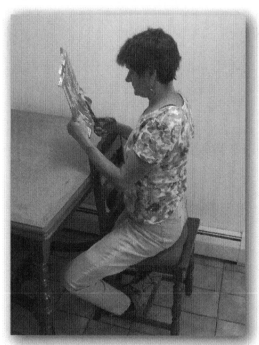

6. Straddling a chair turned backwards can provide support for both arms and legs.

* A rocking chair, glider, or hammock can provide calming movement that helps some children focus. An inexpensive option is to suspend a sheet under a table to make a hammock in a private sensory space (see photo 7). The ends of the sheet are tied tightly together on top of the table. This enjoyable position may motivate some children to participate in hand activities. For others it provides a safe retreat when sensations become overwhelming.

7. This hammock is made by suspending a sheet under a table.

* Offer the option to sit on or lean against a vibrating cushion. Electric or battery-powered cushions are available in health and beauty departments or through special education catalogs. An inexpensive option is to place an electric toothbrush or hand-held massager inside a small cushion.

WEIGHTED VESTS, COLLARS, LAP BAGS, OR WRIST WEIGHTS

For children who find deep pressure calming, wearing a weighted vest or other heavy object may help them self-regulate and better tolerate hand activities. After 20 or 30 minutes the body gets used to the weight, and the benefits wear off; therefore, use weighted equipment for limited periods. Consult an occupational therapist to determine the best weight and wearing schedule. For children who avoid hand activities, I like to pair the positive experience of weighted materials with a brief fine motor task followed by a fun movement such as marching.

A heavy blanket or sleeping bag draped around the shoulders is another means to provide beneficial heavy pressure. Long socks or tights filled with sand can also be draped around the shoulders. Placing the sand inside sealable plastic bags before slipping it inside the socks minimizes sand leakage. Purchasing or making a weighted blanket is another option. The Resource section provides links to online directions.

A weighted lap bag is another choice that is easy to make: simply fill sealable plastic bags with sand, then place them inside a pillowcase. The sweatshirt shown in photo 8 has bags of sand sewn into the sleeves. Children may wrap the sweatshirt sleeves over their shoulders while seated. Alternatively, place a cushion inside the trunk of the sweatshirt; have the child sit on it and fold the weighted sleeves over the lap.

Some children experience better focus and body awareness when wearing wrist weights or using heavy balls or beanbags during activities. Young children may enjoy weighted stuffed animals: simply remove the stuffing material and replace with a bag of sand. Other adaptations include

- wearing a backpack filled with bags of sand
- placing small bags of sand inside the many pockets of a fishing vest
- making rings to stack by filling a sock with sand and sewing the ends together
- filling boxes with sand to use in stacking or construction activities

8. A sweatshirt with weighted sleeves offers deep pressure.

FIDGET TOOLS

Many children and adults focus better when fidgeting with something; for example, jingling coins in one's pocket, pulling a zipper up and down, or tapping a pencil. Grasping and manipulating objects in these ways may be calming, alerting, or both. Many commercial "sensory" products are available to provide this kind of hand stimulation. Fidget tools may be considered primarily a sensory fidget or quiet fidget tool.

Sensory fidget tools provide deep pressure stimulation to muscles and joints as they are pulled, squeezed, or pushed. Choosing sensory fidget tools requires individualization and some trial and error—one child may quietly pull on a stretchy toy while another might shoot it at peers. Possible sensory fidget tools include these:

1. Stretchy book covers, socks, coiled bracelets or key chains, rubber bands, or elastic hair bands. Children may enjoy stretching elastics around a ball of crunched-up paper to make a rubber-band ball.
2. Squeezing putty, modeling clay, or stress balls. You can make your own squeeze ball by pushing play dough inside a large, strong balloon. Knot the balloon, then double its strength by inserting it inside a second balloon. This is easier to do if you cut the knot end off of the second balloon.
3. A kneadable eraser is enjoyable to mold and use, and may appeal to older children who do not want to look different than their peers.
4. Attach a strip of Velcro hook or loop fastener to a table or desk. Then attach pieces of Velcro fastener to a couple of blocks or similar objects. The child can repeatedly attach and remove them while working.
5. Toys that make sounds, light up, or vibrate when squeezed, pulled, or pushed may be especially fun and stimulating.

Some sensory fidget tools are specifically designed for children who also seek oral stimulation. Some products are worn around the neck and designed as safer alternatives to chewing on hands or clothing (see the Resources).

Quiet fidget tools fill the sensory needs of children who focus better while quietly moving their fingers. A quiet fidget tool might be a smooth stone, pen cap, marble, strand of beads, or paper clip. Advantages of quiet fidget tools are that they are generally not disruptive to other children and can be easily replaced when lost. A child can easily put the object down when engaged in a hand activity, or may be able to tuck it under the ring and pinky fingers while doing puzzles or even writing.

Summary: D. Strategies for Sensory Modulation Disorders

   I. Sensory-based strategies for sensory modulation disorders may involve alternative seating/positioning, weighted materials, or fidget tools.

  II. Varying children's head position and exploring seating options may provide sensory stimulation that motivates them to engage in hand activities.

 III. Wearing or using weighted materials provides deep pressure sensory stimulation. This may help children to better self-regulate in order to engage in hand activities.

 IV. Fidget tools are objects that are grasped or manipulated to promote calmness, alertness, or engagement.

  V. Sensory fidget tools are pulled, squeezed, or pushed. These movements provide deep pressure stimulation to muscles and joints.

 VI. Quiet fidget tools are small, common household objects that a child finds calming to grasp or manipulate, such as a pen cap.

VII. Some children may be more willing to engage in hand activities while grasping a quiet fidget tool, such as rolling a smooth stone or kneading a soft eraser.

E. The Impact of Sensory-Based Motor Disorders

Many children with autism have the type of SPD called a *sensory-based motor disorder.*

Sensory-based motor disorders consist of two subtypes:

- Postural disorders: Children with postural disorders have difficulties to stabilize their bodies while using their hands

* <u>Dyspraxia:</u> Children with dyspraxia have difficulties to plan and perform motor tasks.

Many children with sensory-based motor disorders have challenges in both of these areas and have decreased **body awareness**. A child with poor body awareness might sit on top of, instead of next to, another child, have difficulty fitting his arm into a sleeve, or use so much force on a spoon that he splatters food on his clothing when scooping. Children with dyspraxia often do not stabilize materials when working- such as steadying the paper while writing. They may not have developed a preference for the right or left hand by grade school. Also, they often avoid reaching from one side of the body to the other. I will discuss strategies to address these concerns in detail later in this chapter.

WHAT IS BODY AWARENESS?

Imagine yourself on the moon wearing a bulky, awkward spacesuit. You are wearing thick gloves so you can't feel the moon's surface very well. You can't tell how rough, hard, or smooth the rocks feel. Since you weigh one-sixth of your usual weight, you have to use much less force when walking or picking up rocks. It's easy to accidentally use too much force for a task.

The astronauts had lots of preparation for these conditions back on earth. Still, when they landed on the moon they looked like kids learning how to move their bodies, literally, in space. Children with poor body awareness have similar challenges. Even though they have spent all their years on earth, they often struggle to accurately interpret relationships between their body and objects. This is common in children with ASD.

Body awareness refers to how our brains interpret and use sensory information from touch and movement to know

* where our arms and legs are in space, and
* how our body parts are moving in relation to each other, the environment, and objects.

Children with decreased body awareness may touch the walls while walking down the hallway to help them judge distances or they may depend on their vision to guide their hands while buttoning a sweater. Children with poor body awareness and coordination often benefit from the sensory strategies I described earlier, such as use of adapted seating and positioning and weighted materials. They also benefit from activities that are **multisensory-**or engage several senses, require using force, and adapted to promote success.

COORDINATING THE RIGHT AND LEFT SIDES

Most typically developing children show a preference for one hand or the other by the time they enter kindergarten, although it is not abnormal to develop **hand dominance** as late as six or seven years of age.[11] Children develop coordination between the right and left sides of the body when the right and left halves of their brain- called the **brain hemispheres-** are communicating efficiently. Many children with SPD, especially those with dyspraxia, have difficulty with coordinating the two sides of their body, especially to perform complex tasks such as braiding hair or knitting. Because the right and left halves of their brain may not communicate well, these children may develop hand dominance (right- or left-handedness) at an older age than is typical, or not at all.

Let's take a brief look at the relationship between brain hemispheres and hand dominance. Each hemisphere controls the opposite side of the body—the left hemisphere controls the right side, and vice versa. One hemisphere of the brain is typically dominant, and people develop greater skill on the body side opposite the dominant hemisphere. Thus, someone with a dominant right hemisphere is typically left-handed. Most people are right-handed, have greater skill on the right side of the body and have a dominant left hemisphere.

The term **hand preference** is sometimes used to mean hand dominance. However, hand dominance is the result of **brain specialization.** This means that certain skills- like language- develop in one hemisphere rather than the other and that one hemisphere becomes dominant with the opposite side of the body becoming more skilled.

There are other reasons why a child may prefer one hand over the other. For example, Thomas may be left-handed but use his right hand to cut because he was given right-handed scissors or he imitated his right-handed teacher. Some children switch hands when one hand gets tired or when they are searching for a more comfortable way to grasp a tool. Modifying tasks may help them to use their dominant hand consistently. For example, a fat pencil that is easier to grasp may reduce hand switching due to fatigue.

It is important to develop hand dominance because using the same hand consistently for specific tasks helps develop proficiency. Try writing with your non-preferred hand and you can see what I mean. Some children develop what is called **crossed** or **mixed dominance.** This means that they use different hands for specific skills. For example, Claude became adept at using his right hand to write and his left hand to throw a ball. This was not a problem because he practiced each skill consistently with the same hand. Thus, he became very good at throwing with the left hand and writing with the right.

Imagine a line that runs down your body, dividing it into right and left sides. This is called the **midline.** Many children with SPD avoid reaching across midline, or even bringing their hands together at midline. Children with poor coordination between the right and left sides of the body may also have difficulty using their hands together to stabilize materials and to discriminate right from left. Here are examples:

- Heather does not stabilize materials with her left **helper hand** while using her right **worker hand.** For example, she does not hold her bowl while scooping soup. Sometimes she refuses to use her left hand at all.
- Gail wants to drink from a cup located left of her midline. She picks up the cup with her left hand and transfers it to her right hand. It would be much more efficient for her to reach across her body with her right hand to grasp it, but Gail avoids crossing midline.

* Renee does not cross midline when drawing a line inside a maze path. Instead she rotates the paper in order to follow the path.
* Allen does not consistently discriminate right and left on his body and in the environment. He makes frequent letter reversals when reading or writing, like mixing up *b* and *d*.

Summary: E. The Impact of Sensory-Based Motor Disorders

   I. Sensory-based motor disorders are a type of SPD that consists of subtypes: (1) postural disorders, and (2) dyspraxia.

  II. Body awareness enables us to interpret where our arms and legs are and how they are moving in relation to our body and nearby objects.

 III. Using the same hand consistently for specific skills enables children to practice and develop proficiency in that skill.

 IV. Children with dyspraxia may have difficulties using their hands together, crossing midline or discriminating right and left. They may reverse letters or words (*was* for *saw*) and may develop a hand dominance later than is typical or not at all.

F. Strategies for Sensory-Based Motor Disorders

Toy manufacturers know that children love multisensory games and products that engage several senses. That is why some ring stackers and puzzles play music, baby toys may vibrate, markers may be scented, and some balls make giggly sounds when thrown. Multisensory products like these may help children better understand where objects are in relation to their bodies and how parts fit together. Many children find that multisensory and resistive activities help them to tolerate touch better so that they can engage in hand activities.

ADAPTING HAND ACTIVITIES TO BE RESISTIVE

Hand activities that involve squeezing, pushing, or pulling provide deep pressure sensory stimulation to muscles, joints, and tendons. These activities are called **resistive** because they require force. Pulling a heavy door open or playing tug-of-war are resistive because the arms and shoulders use a lot of force. Resistive activities such as squeezing a hole puncher, coloring over sandpaper with a crayon, or ripping cardboard use the smaller muscles in the hands while the arm and shoulder muscles work to stabilize the body.

Resistive activities feel good—not only children but many adults love to pull, squeeze, and push with their hands and bodies. We see this during pillow fights and wrestling matches, or when people squeeze balls sold to relieve stress. There are many simple resistive activities that use the arms and shoulders. Examples are

* using the hands to roll a large ball up and down a wall while standing or kneeling
* "painting" a garage or other outdoor structure with water using a heavy brush or roller
* shoveling snow or sand
* dragging a blanket that is holding another child or a pet
* pushing a heavy bag suspended from a branch. Try filling the bag with sand, birdseed, or water balloons.

Resistive activities using the hands are plentiful:

* Commercial toys—such as Legos, Tinker Toys, K'nex, or Mr. Potato Head—require children to use force to connect and separate small parts.

- Many kitchen gadgets are resistive. Think of rolling pins, cookie cutters, garlic presses, egg beaters, or flour sifters. Some children may be motivated to use these tools to create an edible treat.
- Forcefully separating strips of Velcro fastener from backings often motivates children because it provides both fun sounds and forceful pulling.

Here are a few of my most popular resistive activities.

Feeding the Hungry Harry Ball

Make "Hungry Harry" (see photo 9) by cutting a mouth in a tennis ball and drawing on a face. Children must squeeze the ball hard to open his mouth wide enough to feed him small objects such as coins. To increase the challenge, embed the "food" in putty. Removing the small objects from putty in order to feed Hungry Harry provides an additional resistive activity.

9. Hungry Harry is a squeeze toy made from a tennis ball.

Children should not be expected to have the hand strength to squeeze Hungry Harry until around age four or five. The longer the mouth opening, the easier it is to squeeze it open, so you can adjust the length according to the child's ability.

Velcro Bottles or Containers

Young children around 18 to 36 months of age, and older children functioning at this level, often love to remove toys attached to a container with Velcro hook-and-loop fastener. I have used detergent and dishwasher soap bottles of all different sizes and shapes, as well as commercial shape sorters like the one shown in photo 10. This activity develops eye-hand coordination as children insert the objects, and it works best when they stabilize the container with one hand.

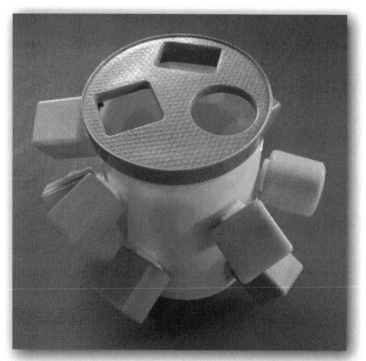

10. The shapes are attached to this shape sorter with Velcro fastener.

Velcro bottle activities are very easy to make. Simply cover a bottle with many small pieces of hook Velcro. Then attach a piece of loop Velcro to toys that can be attached, pulled off, and then inserted. Use longer pieces of Velcro to increase resistance. Closely supervise children or avoid using toys that are small enough to create a choking hazard.

Attaching the toys to the bottle instead of placing them on the table may also help children focus better—toys scattered on the table can be distracting. Many children focus even better when an electric toothbrush is inserted inside the container.

Resistive Ring Stacks and Stringing

Both ring stacks and stringing activities can be adapted to require the use of force. Any dowel, sturdy tube, or piece of PVC pipe can function as a ring stack when wedged inside a bottle or box. The one shown in photo 11 is made by wedging a foam swimming noodle inside an opening in a

11. This homemade ring stack is resistive and vibrates, creating an irresistible multisensory experience.

juice bottle. There is a motorized pen pushed into the top of the noodle to create vibration. The rings are cut with small enough openings that they require force to push them down the noodle. I cut the rings for this activity out of plastic container lids and detergent bottles, but you can also buy rings at a craft or hardware store.

Smaller rings can be used to make resistive stringing activities using thick cord instead of string. I have tied the ends of men's ties together, and then made additional knots in them. The child has to use force to push the rings down over the knots. Traditional stringing beads can be challenging for children with poor eye-hand coordination. However, stringing rings or doughnut shapes makes the materials much easier to grasp and manipulate. I have made many variations by tying objects to the inserting end of the cord so that the child must use force to get the ring over it. Try using

* a children's electric toothbrush. Cover it with duct tape so that children don't think it goes inside the mouth (see photo 12)
* a ball that is squeezed or lights up
* toys that squeak when squeezed

12. Use an electric toothbrush to add vibration to resistive stringing.

Note that all of these activities require using the two hands together in order to stabilize or manipulate materials. Children can be ingenious in finding ways to perform tasks using only one hand. However, adapting materials to be heavier, longer, or bulkier; to vibrate; or to require force will help children to coordinate using their right and left hands together.

ADAPTING TO MAKE SUCCESS EASY AND FREQUENT

You have learned how to adapt ring stacks and stringing activities to be fun and provide sensory stimulation. This is especially important when teaching children who avoid using their hands due to past failures. Let's look at ways to adapt the following activities so that success becomes easier and more frequent:

* pegboards
* shape sorters
* lacing boards
* buttoning
* cutting with scissors

Sensory Pegboards

A child trying to place small pegs in a pegboard may knock pegs out while attempting to insert more. I designed the "sensory pegboard" (see photo 13) to avoid this problem. The board is made by wedging one cardboard box inside another then covering it with adhesive paper. Cut holes through the top surface and apply tape around them to create color contrast and smooth edges. Small plastic bottles serve as pegs. They can be recycled from juice or contact lens supplies. Filling them with water adds weight, and adding sparkly items like glitter to the water makes them look pretty when shaken. These weighted "pegs" don't easily fall out as children add more to the board.

13. The sensory pegboard is designed so that the pegs won't easily fall out.

Adapted Shape Sorters

Use large detergent or dishwasher soap bottles with handles to make shape sorters. The handle encourages the child to stabilize the bottle with one hand while inserting objects with the other. The homemade sorter shown in photo 14 has slots for inserting thick cards or pieces of plastic.

You may cut a long horizontal slit near the bottom for removing objects that are too large to remove through the bottle's pouring end. The large screw caps make it easy to store materials, and children can also practice opening and closing them.

Modifications: Cut square holes for inserting blocks or rectangular holes for inserting dominoes. Many children enjoy this activity when a motor is placed inside the bottle so that it vibrates.

14. A homemade shape sorter can be adapted to
suit a child's needs and preferences.

Adapted Lacing Board

The lacing boards sold in stores typically have many small holes and use flimsy string. Flimsy string is difficult to control and a large number of holes can be overwhelming. Commercial lacing boards are often frustrating for a child who has difficulty with eye-hand coordination.

It is easy to make your own lacing board out of cardboard or plastic. The one shown in photo 15 is cut out of a detergent bottle. Choose a size and number of holes that suit your child's abilities. Tie thick cord or aquarium tubing to the starter hole. These boards are so easy to make, I

15. This lacing board is easy to make and use.

suggest cutting several in letter shapes so that they can be used to spell words after being laced.

Adapted Buttoning

Fastening and unfastening buttons is easier when using extra-large "buttons" and "button squares." The button squares consist of a piece of fabric with a button sewn to the center and a separate piece of fabric with a slit cut in the center. Start out using very large real or simulated buttons and progress to using smaller ones. You can make simulated buttons in any size by punching two holes into a large plastic circle (see photo 16). Sew the circle onto one piece of fabric. Then the fabric with the slit can be buttoned onto the button square.

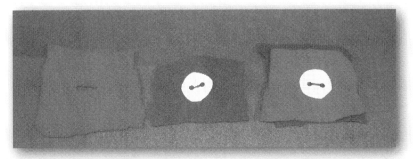

16. Large button squares are easier to manipulate than buttons on clothing.

Buttoning clothing you are wearing can be challenging because it is difficult to see what you are doing. Children can practice using button squares on a table or in their laps so that they can watch what they're doing.

Some children may find a "buttoning board" easier to use because the board stabilizes the "buttons." To make a buttoning board

1. sew buttons or plastic circles onto fabric
2. then sew or tape the fabric tightly around a large piece of cardboard or plastic (see photo 17).
3. Cut buttonholes in scraps of fabric that the child can attach to the board.

17. Attaching fabric squares to a buttoning board.

Another adaptation that develops buttoning skills is to string pieces of plastic or fabric onto cord that has a button shape attached to the tip (see photo 18).The child then inserts the button tip though plastic pieces with slit-like openings. As their skill develops children may string fabric pieces instead of plastic ones. Experiment to find a button and hole size that your child can use successfully. Gradually increase the challenge by making both smaller.

18. Button stringing helps develop dexterity to use real buttons.

Cutting with Scissors

Cutting requires two hands—the worker hand to use the scissors and the helper hand to hold the paper while cutting. Many children neglect to move the helper hand as they cut along a line. Placing stickers along the side of a piece of paper shows the child where to move the thumb as the cutting hand moves upward. You can point to or name the next picture the thumb should cover to cue the child to move the hand.

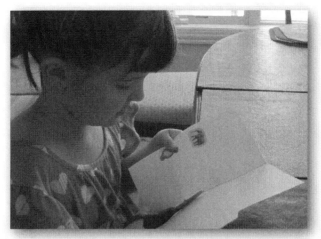

19. Stickers guide this girl where to place her helper hand while cutting.

Note that the girl in photo 19 is cutting across a manila folder rather than construction paper. Thick paper folders give children increased sensory feedback because they need to use more force, plus it is less likely to rip than thin paper.

Tape one end of a long strip of paper to a wall at about the child's head height (see photo 20). The child then cuts in an upward direction along the strip. This helps position the wrist correctly with the thumb facing upwards.

20. Paper taped to a wall helps position the wrist in correct cutting position.

Buckling and Weaving

Weaving is the process of making cloth by using two sets of thread that go over and under each other. It is a wonderful process that develops strong fingers and the dexterity needed for opening and closing buckles. The following two adaptations develop dexterity by weaving plastic rather than cloth. The practice "belt" shown in photo 21 is easier to manipulate than a leather or fabric belt since the plastic is very firm. The belt is made by cutting around a large round container such as a bleach bottle. Cut one end a bit narrower than the other and cut two parallel slits in the wider end. The narrow end can be woven under and over the two notches to "buckle the belt." The "belt" in the photo has strips of duct tape to create color contrast and indicate which end to grasp when starting to buckle.

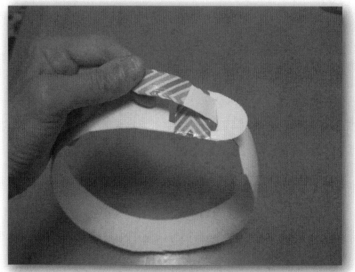

21. The child weaves the end of this plastic belt through notches to "buckle" it.

A variety of notched shapes can be woven onto the same plastic belt, as shown in photo 22. This activity is fun, because children can choose colors and shapes to sequence a pattern, and they have lots of opportunity for manipulation practice.

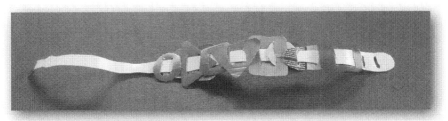

22. A sequence of different shapes can be woven onto the belt strip.

STRATEGIES TO PROMOTE RIGHT-LEFT COORDINATION

Sensory stimulation that promotes coordination between the two sides of the body begins during infancy. For example, when positioned on their tummies, babies learn to look, and eventually roll, toward each side. Crawling is a very important developmental skill because it promotes coordination between the right and left sides of the body.

Older children develop right-left coordination by jumping, propelling a scooter, pedaling a tricycle, and pumping their legs to swing. Going down slides, riding merry-go-rounds, swimming, sledding, and rolling down hills all provide deep pressure sensory stimulation. Activities like these develop coordination between the right and left sides of the body—including the right and left hands.

If you are concerned about your child's left-right coordination, here are a few helpful tips:

1. Do not assume that a child under age five years of age has a hand preference. Position or offer materials at midline so that the child can choose which hand to use.
2. Offer lots of activities that require using both hands equally: ripping paper, rolling modeling dough snakes, using a rolling pin, or playing tug-of-war.
3. Once a child over five years of age demonstrates a hand preference, encourage consistent use of that hand. This is especially important for highly skilled tasks such as writing.

4. Avoid hand switching due to fatigue by reducing the workload, offering breaks, or adapting the activity. For example, self-opening scissors require less strength to squeeze.
5. Offer older children hand tools such as hole punchers, staplers, pencil sharpeners, or carpentry tools that require using force. Using these tools sends sensory information to the muscles and joints that helps children to identify which hand is more skilled.
6. Teach children the terms *worker hand* and *helper hand*. The worker hand does the movement—such as cutting—while the helper hand provides stabilization—such as holding the paper.
7. Watch for signs of crossed or mixed dominance. If they appear, encourage the child to use the same hand consistently for the same tasks.

1-2-3 PULL!

I love my 1-2-3 PULL! because it provides great sensory stimulation to the hand muscles. To make a 1-2-3 PULL!, cut holes at the same height on the front and back of a detergent bottle. Thread a thick strip of fabric through both holes. Make sure that the fabric is thick enough or the holes small enough so that it takes force to pull. Cut each end of the fabric to be thin enough to tie around a ring as shown in photo 23. Attach a ring to each end of the fabric. I made these rings by cutting around the threaded pieces of dishwasher soap bottles, but you can buy rings from a hardware or craft store. Repeat these steps to make more rings to pull. I suggest making no more than three so that the cords do not become tangled.

First have the child grasp the bottle handle with the left hand while pulling the rings with the right. Then reverse the bottle so that the child grasps the handle with the right hand and pulls the rings with the left. The child will alternate which hand stabilizes the bottle and which pulls, thereby helping her to discover which hand has better control.

23. The 1-2-3 PULL! toy is a favorite.

STRATEGIES TO PROMOTE CROSSING MIDLINE

Typically developing children naturally cross midline during play and functional activities. This is not a skill that parents usually teach, which is why you've probably never heard the term before. Recall that children with dyspraxia or other types of SPD may avoid crossing midline.

Seven-year-old Pedro reached for markers using whichever hand was closest to them, and then used that hand to color. He didn't attempt to stabilize the paper with his opposite hand. Observing this, the teacher consulted with the school OT, Leila. Leila recommended that he practice forming large circles on a whiteboard. She offered him a marker posi-tioned directly in front of him, at midline. He grasped it with his left hand, suggesting this hand might be dominant. Leila gently held his right arm at his side while he drew large circles on the board.

Next, Leila placed her hand on top of his to guide his movements **(hand-over-hand assistance)***. With this help Pedro was able to trace over large diagonal crosses and horizontal figure-eights without switch-ing hands.*

Leila also recommended activities to help Pedro strengthen his hands, especially his fingers, so that he didn't switch the marker from hand to hand due to fatigue. His teacher tried the 1-2-3 PULL! activity (described earlier) and realized that Pedro's left hand had better control than his right when pulling the rings. This observation reinforced the idea that he was left-hand dominant.

Pedro had dyspraxia. This showed up in a cluster of symptoms such as late development of a hand preference, decreased coordination, avoidance of crossing midline, and reluctance to hold materials steady with his helper hand. The 1-2-3 PULL toy was especially beneficial because Pedro had to hold the handle while pulling, and the resistance gave extra sensory feedback.

The following activities offer other ways to promote crossing midline:

1. Find two containers of different colors (such as red and blue) and beanbags to match. Place the red beanbags on the child's left and the red container on the child's right, and vice-versa for the blue. Instruct the child to insert the red beanbags into the red container with the right hand, and the blue beanbags into the blue container with the left hand. If the child tries to switch hands instead of reaching across midline, give a verbal reminder to use one hand, or gently hold down the opposite hand.
2. Ask the child to touch her right knee with her left hand. Repeat with various body parts. Reverse by showing her how to use the right hand to touch named body parts on the left side of her body.

3. Place peel-off stickers on one side of the child's body. Have him remove each sticker using the hand opposite the stickers. Reverse side and hand used.

4. Twister is a commercially available game consisting of a mat with different colored circles and a spinner. Players spin to determine which hand or foot has to be placed on which color of circle. It's a fun way to practice crossing midline while getting tied up in knots.

5. Cover a large vertical surface, such as paper taped to a wall, with large circles and infinity signs (sideways 8s, ∞). Show the child how to grasp a marker with both hands and trace over the shapes. Now repeat having the child use only the left hand, then only the right hand.

6. Suspend a ball about shoulder height. Have the child bat at the ball with a long tube. Initially have the child hold the tube with both hands. Next repeat with only the left hand, then only the right.

7. With the child sitting at a table, scatter letter blocks or tiles in front of her. Ask the child to find and line up each letter in alphabetical order (see photo 24). Direct the child to alternate the hand used to pick up the next letter in the alphabet—*A* with the right hand, *B* with the left, *C* with the right, and so on. It will at times be necessary to reach across midline.

24. Arranging scattered letter tiles in alphabetical
order requires crossing midline.

Summary: F. Strategies for Sensory-Based Motor Disorders

    I. Sensory-based motor disorders are a subtype of SPD. They consist of postural disorders and dyspraxia.

   II. Body awareness enables us to interpret where our arms and legs are and how they are moving in relation to our body and nearby objects.

 III. Promote success by use of adapted seating and positioning, multisensory activities, and resistive activities that give sensory feedback.

 IV. Provide activities that involve pushing, pulling, or squeezing. These are called "resistive" because they require using force.

  V. Simplify activities by making materials larger or sturdier, creating color contrast, and/or reducing the steps involved.

 VI. Encourage children to do lots of activities that use both hands equally, such as ripping cardboard, as well as activities that require stabilization, such as the 1-2-3 PULL! toy. These help children to discover or develop a hand preference.

VII. Provide fine-motor activities that involve reaching across midline with each hand and with both hands together.

G. Sensory Discrimination Disorder

Sensory discrimination disorder is the last of the six SPD subtypes. It refers to abilities to differentiate various sensory stimuli such as temperatures, textures, and colors. For review, we have the following eight sensory systems and any of them may be impacted by a sensory discrimination disorder:

Sensory discrimination disorders

1. <u>Visual:</u> Sense of sight
2. <u>Auditory:</u> Sense of hearing

3. <u>Gustatory:</u> Sense of taste
4. <u>Olfactory:</u> Sense of smell
5. <u>Tactile:</u> Sense of touch
6. <u>Proprioception:</u> Sense of position in space
7. <u>Vestibular:</u> Sense of balance
8. <u>Interoception</u>: sense of internal regulation

Children with sensory discrimination disorders often overreact to sensations they see, hear, taste, or feel. You have learned that this is called *sensory defensiveness.* Sensory defensiveness can impact any of the senses. However, it is the tactile sense that is most important for learning to grasp and manipulate objects. Children with **tactile defensiveness** (an overreaction to touch sensations) who have avoided early touch experiences, such as grasping a rattle, may be slow to learn about how objects differ in texture, size, weight, shape, or other attributes. These children may manipulate objects in an awkward and inefficient manner.

Many of the same strategies that help children with sensory modulation challenges also help children who are sensitive to touch and movement. Strategies include tummy positioning early in infancy, deep pressure and resistive activities, alternatives to messy play, and use of multisensory activities.

The Importance of "Tummy Time"

Babies with sensory defensiveness may cry when placed on their tummies because they dislike the sensation of gravity pulling their weight downward. When babies are in the prone position on their bellies, they have to work extra hard to lift their head and chest off the floor. This is especially difficult for babies who have low muscle tone or poor postural control. Parents naturally will avoid a position that appears to upset their baby. As a result these babies don't experience the important position called **tummy time.** The prone position provides heavy-pressure sensory stimulation to muscles and joints as babies support their body weight on forearms, hands, and later hands and knees when crawling. Babies who miss out on these experiences may become overly sensitive to touch on their palms. They may also appear to have

- undeveloped hand muscles and flat hand arches
- unusual ways of grasping objects, using just the fingertips instead of grasping within the palms
- poor hand strength and manipulation skills. These make it challenging to grasp a rope swing tightly or control a pencil.

There are several factors that have likely contributed to a decrease in tummy time over the past couple of decades. Pediatricians began the "Back to Sleep" campaign in 1994 because babies who sleep prone are at greater risk for sudden infant death syndrome (SIDS). Modern-day babies spend much of their time in infant seats, car seats, and other seating devices, which limit opportunities to move freely on the floor. It is difficult to say which came first—sensory defensiveness caused by lack of tummy time or lack of tummy time because babies don't like it. Regardless, it is important to encourage *supervised* periods of tummy time beginning as young as possible, and to continue with prone activities throughout the child's life.

Six-month-old Dianna absolutely hated to lie on her tummy. Her mom, Eleanor, wasn't too concerned. As the youngest of four children, Dianna was often in

- *the van's car seat while Eleanor took siblings to sports*
- *a cart while Eleanor shopped*
- *a stroller when Eleanor took her daily walk with other moms, and*
- *in a high chair while Eleanor cooked dinner*

In addition, with four kids running about, Eleanor felt that the house was not particularly clean. She preferred placing her baby in a walker or "Exersaucer"—a fancy positioning device the baby sits in while surrounded by toys—rather than on the floor. Dianna never crawled! However, her parents were delighted when at 12 months of age she not only walked, she started running.

Actually, Dianna began running because she had poor postural control and low muscle tone. It was actually easier for her to keep moving than to sit or stand in one place. By the time Dianna was two years old, Eleanor was concerned that her daughter often bumped into things, refused to touch anything gooey—including food—and seemed to have no hand skills other than throwing objects.

Here are a few ideas that might have helped Dianna tolerate, maybe even enjoy, tummy time:

1. Introduce tummy position early, preferably soon after birth. The earlier you start, the more natural it will seem to your baby. Begin with a few seconds and gradually increase to minutes and up to half an hour. During the first few weeks babies can get used to gravity pulling their head, neck, and body downward while napping on a parent's chest.
2. Encourage older babies to lift their heads to look upward and to the left and right. Provide lots of fun distractions, such as looking into mirrors or at colorful toys, lights, pets, and of course, loved ones.
3. Don't be afraid to place your baby on the floor. Experiment with different textured surfaces such as a shag rug, sheepskin, or *busy blanket* (shown in photo 25). These are sold with sensory toys attached.
4. Position a rolled-up towel or small cushion under the baby's chest. This makes it easier for the baby to hold up the head.
5. Position the baby on top of a small bolster or ball to provide a gentle rocking movement.
6. Try using the "football hold" once a baby has enough control to hold the head steady. Dr. Anne Zachry describes this position:

Hold the baby "belly down on your forearm with his head resting near the inside of your elbow. The baby is held close to the adult's body making him feel safe and secure, and this position encourages him to lift and turn his head to see what is going on around him."[12] Between four and six months of age, a typically developing baby is able to hold her head up without support while receiving deep pressure touch from Mom's hands and body.

25. Placing babies on a "busy blanket" with toys encourages them to lift their heads.

Getting Babies Grasping

Typically developing six-month-old Frank is grasping and shaking toys that fit inside his palm. He is also learning to clap and bang objects together. He especially loves to throw them to see where they end up and if his dad will retrieve them. This turns into a great back-and-forth social game that Frank and his dad love to play, again and again.

When babies avoid grasping with the whole hand, they miss out on the type of social, cognitive, and sensory learning that Frank is enjoying. Here are a few strategies that might motivate babies to grasp:

1. Explore which textures your baby prefers and avoids. Perhaps your baby does not like soft, fluffy stuffed animals—even if you did get dozens at the baby shower. Children with ASD often prefer plastic or wooden objects.

2. Explore placing baby toys that vary in size, shape, and weight inside the baby's palms.

3. Try stuffing a sock with objects that are interesting to feel, such as marbles, sand, pennies, bells, foam, packing peanuts, plastic bags, or a combination of these. (Sew the sock securely closed to avoid choking hazards.) Sewing the ends of the sock together creates a ring that the baby can fit his hand inside to grasp.

4. Look for toys that are *multisensory*, or appeal to several senses at the same time. For example, some wonderful toys make exciting sounds, have flashing lights, and vibrate. I have found that spring-loaded toys that vibrate when pulled are effective because they give sensory stimulation from both pulling and vibration.

5. Combine the act of grasping with something the baby loves, possibly movement. For example, place the baby in a stationary swing. Each time baby grasps a rattle, give the swing a push. Stop the movement when the baby releases the toy and begin the game again.

Toddlers and older children benefit from putting weight on their hands even long after they learn to walk and run. Supporting their body weight on their hands provides heavy-pressure sensory stimulation that helps children tolerate touch while also developing coordination between the right and left sides of the body. Encourage children to

* crawl through tunnels
* propel a scooter board while in prone position using their hands

- lie prone over a bolster or ball, and rock back and forth, pushing off the floor with their hands
- lie prone on a low swing and push off the ground with their hands to make the swing move
- wheelbarrow-walk (see photo 26). Some children will have enough postural control to walk on their hands with someone holding their ankles. Other children will need to be supported at the thighs or hips.

26. This girl bears weight on her hands while wheelbarrow-walking.

OFFERING ALTERNATIVES TO MESSY PLAY

Children with tactile defensiveness generally avoid touching paint, glue, toothpaste, moist foods, gooey objects in general, and even water. It is especially important for these children to have the freedom to make a mess as they explore the sensory qualities of objects.

Three-year-old Helen came to her first day of preschool wearing a yellow dress with a big bow tied in the back, sandals, and red nail polish. She was very concerned about messing up her French braid and clothing, so she refused to run, go near the sandbox, or touch paint. She cried when she smelled the modeling dough. Helen preferred to sit in one place for a long time, and the farther away she was from other children who might jostle her, the calmer she seemed.

Helen's mom agreed to dress her in shorts and sneakers, and her occupational therapist focused on deep pressure/tactile activities. Helen applied glue using a paintbrush so that she could avoid touching it. She preferred using a motorized pen instead of messy markers to scribble. Helen refused to touch finger paint, so her teacher filled heavy-duty resealable plastic bags with paint. Helen could press the bags with her fingers to form circles. These adaptations enabled Helen to experience **messy play** *on her own terms—without actually making a mess. Eventually, Helen began using a rolling pin and plastic knife to play with modeling dough scented with applesauce.*

Alternatives to messy play—such as scribbling on a plastic bag filled with paint—are not meant to replace tactile sensory activities but rather to introduce them in a tolerable fashion while gradually introducing new textures. This is very important because children with ASD often refuse to eat many types of foods. Exposure to touching a variety of textures can help expand their food repertoire.

Summary: G. Sensory Discrimination Disorder

I. Sensory discrimination disorder is one of the six subtypes of SPD. Children with this subtype have difficulties discriminating sensations and have atypical responses to sensory stimuli.

II. Children with sensory defensiveness over-react to sensory stimuli.

III. Tactile defensiveness is a sensitivity to touch. A child with this condition may refuse to touch certain textures or grasp objects, or may over-react when touched.

IV. Children with tactile defensiveness may have undeveloped hand muscles and unusual ways of grasping objects. They may also resist being positioned on their tummies.

V. Tummy time provides important sensory stimulation to skin, muscles, joints, and the vestibular sensory system (which influences balance).

VI. Tummy time promotes lifting the head and supporting weight on forearms and later hands, which helps a baby to build strong neck, shoulder, arm, and hand muscles.

VII. Supervised periods of tummy time can begin soon after birth.

VIII. Activities that involve putting weight on the hands—such as wheelbarrow-walking—continue to benefit older children. Such activities provide heavy-pressure stimulation to the arms and hands.

IX. Adapt messy play activities so that children can engage in them without touching textures they dislike. Gradually introduce new touch experiences, such as paint, glue or whipped cream.

CHAPTER 3

Functional Vision, Visual Perception, and Hand Skills

● ● ●

Many people with ASD have incredible visual abilities. Some can quickly pick out minute visual differences, nonverbal artists have reproduced detailed scenes from memory, and there are children like Paul:

> *Five-year-old Paul can quickly put together a 500-piece puzzle or move his finger along a complex maze on his IPad. He also has the uncanny ability to find and eat any crumb that lands on the richly patterned carpet. At the same time, he seems to lose everything—from a beloved box of rocks he planned to shine to the shoes he took off at Grandma's house.*
>
> *Paul does not put out his hands to catch a ball. In fact, he ducks when anything is tossed in his direction—even a pillow, rolled-up newspaper, or mittens. When Paul has nothing particular to occupy his hands, he enjoys flicking his fingers up and down near his eyes.*

The popular movie *Rain Man*, based on the true life story of Kim Peek, offers an extreme example of what I call "the paradox." Raymond, as the character with autism is called in the movie, becomes agitated whenever his routines change. He has no idea what to do when burnt toast sets off the smoke alarm. At the same time his visual memory and uncanny ability to count rapidly enable his brother to win big at a Las Vegas poker table. The paradox is that individuals like Raymond and Paul have exceptional visual perceptual abilities that may enable them to become artists, computer geeks, or card sharks. At the same time, however, they frequently experience visual challenges that hinder their social, communication, and hand skills.

Functional Vision, Eyesight, and Visual Perception

Functional Vision is how the brain and eyes work together to use visual information and perform tasks from catching a ball to reading. Eyesight, the ability to see, is one component, but there is so much more to vision. Terms used to describe the ability to see clearly are

- visual acuity
- focusing abilities
- refractive power
- resolving power

Eyesight is expressed as a ratio of 20 feet. Someone with **20/20 eyesight,** or normal visual acuity, has the power to see an object at a distance of 20 feet as clearly as the average person. Someone with 20/100 vision must be as close as 20 feet to see what a person with normal vision can see at 100 feet away.[13] Other aspects of vision include **depth perception**—the ability to coordinate both eyes together to see in three dimensions—and **visual tracking**- the ability to follow a moving object.

Recall from chapter 1 that *visual perception* refers to how the brain uses the information provided by the eyes to interpret what is in the environment. Visual perception is what enables us to distinguish colors, shapes, letters, and words. Little Paul has excellent focusing power. He can see 20/20 on an eye chart and loves to watch ants travel in the dirt; however, he has difficulty catching and throwing objects because his eyes do not work well together. On the other hand, Paul's brain can really quickly make sense of shapes and how they fit together. Thus, Paul has some advanced visual perceptual skills, but he also has certain challenges with functional vision.

Vision Red Flags

Parents shouldn't have to work at making *eye contact* with their baby. For most babies, eye contact with adults happens naturally, lasts for some time, and is fun. Just watch the babies in the supermarket checkout line who stare at complete strangers, inviting them to smile, wave, and make silly faces. A child who avoids eye contact does not necessarily have autism, but this may be a red flag. Some researchers believe that for people with ASD reduced eye contact may be an attempt to self-regulate—or adapt to the visual demands of a situation—rather than a sign of a social abnormality.[14] However, some children with ASD—my son, for example—develop normal eye contact, especially with familiar people.

Early visual attention is key to developing a social skill called **joint attention**. This occurs when adult and baby both focus on the same thing:

> *Nine-month-old Jane follows her daddy's eyes to see what he is looking at. This prompts communication as Daddy points to the bird he is watching and names it. Jane and Daddy are both aware that they are looking at the same object moving in the sky.*

Scientific studies have examined videos taken of children between 12 and 30 months of age at social events. The children who were later diagnosed with ASD showed significantly less joint attention, social engagement, and visual engagement with objects.[15]

Some parents see red flags during their baby's first year that suggest their child may have difficulties with functional vision. Some of these red flags are challenges with

- **visual fixation-** holding one's gaze on a person or object
- visual tracking- following moving objects with the eyes
- depth perception- seeing in three dimensions
- **scanning**- using eye or head movements to search for details, in a room, on a page, or on a computer screen that has many visual elements

- looking quickly back and forth between two objects
- using **isolated eye movements,** which is moving the eyes alone without moving the head. Isolated eye movements are more efficient for looking at nearby objects. Babies typically develop this skill at around six months of age. Older typically developing children use a combination of head and eye movements when looking in a larger visual field and during gross motor activities such as ball games.

Optometrists are the professionals who prescribe eyeglasses or contact lenses to improve eyesight. According to optometrist Randy Schulman, many of the behavioral characteristics associated with ASD involve the visual system, as well as other sensory systems.[16] These symptoms may include

- poor eye contact
- staring at moving lights or spinning objects
- looking at objects with a sideways view—using **peripheral vision** rather than direct gaze.
- when planning to pick up an object, looking at it, then looking away before picking it up

Optometrist Rebecca E. Hutchins describes the skills that may be challenging for children with ASD as the "Seven Fs":[17]

1. Following: using smooth, coordinated eye movements to track a moving object
2. Fixation: gazing at a stationary object
3. Focus: seeing clearly at given distances
4. Fusion: using the eyes together to see in three dimensions
5. Flexibility: looking back and forth between different things
6. Field: the **visual field** is the full breadth of what the eyes can see while staring straight ahead

7. <u>Fatigue</u>: straining the eyes—using peripheral vision is more tiring than using central, or direct gaze.

Developmental optometrists are specialty vision professionals who not only prescribe eyeglasses, but also diagnose and treat disorders that hinder functional vision. Some of the tools a developmental optometrist may recommend are

*   <u>glasses with prism lenses,</u> which help when the image one eye sees is out of line with what the other eye sees
*   <u>color filters,</u> to improve clarity by adjusting the wavelength of light entering the eye
*   <u>occlusion,</u> patching the stronger eye to make the weaker eye work
*   <u>vision therapy exercises,</u> perhaps to help the eyes work together
*   <u>referral to an ophthalmologist,</u> a medical doctor who specializes in eye care- for possible surgery
*   <u>referral to an occupational therapy</u> for evaluation and treatment related to a sensory processing disorder

If you are unsure of your child's visual abilities the first step is to seek an evaluation by an eye-care professional. You can find information on vision and autism, as well as how to find a doctor at the College of Optometrists in Vision Development website, www.covd.org/?page=Autism.

ADAPTATIONS AND ACTIVITIES THAT PROMOTE VISUAL SKILLS

A hospital study of babies in the neonatal intensive care unit showed that those who were later diagnosed with ASD tended to show early, subtle visual differences. At one month of age about 40% of them did not have normal visual tracking for objects, compared to 10.5% of babies who did not get an ASD diagnosis.[18]

In my book *From Rattles to Writing: A Parent's Guide to Hand Skills* I share many strategies that stimulate the visual sensory system, beginning at birth. These strategies cannot prevent autism or other developmental delays, but can help children develop to the best of their abilities.

VISUALLY STIMULATING TOYS

During the first few weeks of life a typically developing baby may gaze at an object or person for only a few seconds before looking away. Here are ways to encourage your baby to gradually gaze for longer periods:

* Gently place your finger inside the baby's palm, then bring his hand near his eyes so he sees what his hand is doing. This will help baby connect what he feels with what he sees.
* Hold a toy or your face about eight inches away from a newborn's face. This is the distance at which a baby focuses best.
* Show the baby pictures or objects with simple, bold black-and-white geometric designs. Babies can more easily discriminate strong contrasts.
* Position a brightly colored toy at midline. Slowly move it a few inches to the left then to the right of midline.

Over the next few months encourage your baby to visually follow your smiling face and objects that are moving greater distances from side to side, up and down, diagonally, and in circles. Tracking tubes designed to develop these skills are available for purchase. They consist of clear tubes with stimulating objects inside, such as beads, bells, or sparkly gems that roll side to side. It is easy to make homemade versions in various sizes, weights, shapes, and visual effects as follows:

1. Fill a small, clear bottle or tube with a few beads or marbles that can roll back and forth.

2. Fill a bottle halfway with water and colorful beads. Add glitter or food coloring.

3. Make a wave bottle by filling a bottle with half water, half mineral oil, and a bit of food coloring. The water and mineral oil do not mix, so they make beautiful waves as the bottle is tilted.

4. Fill a bottle about three-quarters full with water; add a bottle of colored glue (sold in craft stores) and fine glitter. Shake the bottle to make the glitter dance around. The glue makes the glitter take longer to settle to the bottom, and older children may find this calming to watch.

Be sure to secure all bottles tightly and supervise your baby closely to avoid choking risks. Bottle caps may be secured with a glue gun, duct tape, or by tying a strip of fabric around the cap.

Some babies may be more motivated to look at and grasp multisensory objects. Try using toys that

*   produce funny sounds or music
*   have moving parts
*   vibrate or shake
*   light up

Be sure to present toys or faces on the baby's right and left sides to encourage turning the head to both sides, as well as looking straight ahead. This will help baby learn to coordinate looking toward and rolling to each side and eventually reaching with each hand.

Tip: Take your time! Many children take a few moments to process sensory information, including what they see. So don't remove a toy right away if your baby does not immediately seem to be interested. Other children are easily overstimulated and may respond best with gradual and brief introductions to new toys. Observe how your child responds and gear your presentation to your child's learning needs!

Between four and six months of age, a baby typically learns to reach toward toys with both hands, then with one hand. Between six and twelve months of age they typically start to visually inspect toys: They may transfer them back and forth between their hands, or taste, bang, drop, and rotate them to view them from all angles. If your baby does not explore toys in this way, help him to feel and move the toy in front of his face.

Lights to the Rescue

If your child loves lights, take advantage of the following activities to encourage visual attention. Caution: If your child has a seizure disorder check with your physician first.

Light table: You can buy or make a light table to encourage manipulating objects on a surface. To make your own, place a battery-powered light inside a clear plastic container with lid. Cut small openings of different shapes in the lid in order to use the light box as a shape sorter. Children may be more visually engaged when looking at toys—such as pegs and pegboard—placed on top of a light table or light box. In addition, they may be motivated to touch or manipulate them. Here are other ideas:

1. Collect plastic 20-ounce or two-liter soda bottles. Place an activated glow stick inside each one. Then use a ball to bowl over the bottles.
2. Scatter glow sticks inside a play tunnel for your child to gather. These toys remain lit for several hours after being unwrapped. You can buy a tunnel or make your own by draping blankets over chairs or tables.
3. Play catch with balls that light up, have flashing lights, or make funny sounds when squeezed.

Light-up toys: Toddlers and older children who love lights may be motivated to manipulate the following types of commercially available toys:

- ring stacks that flash lights and play music when rings are stacked on them (such as the Light Up Lion Stacker by Fisher-Price)
- toys that light up when a button is pushed (such as the Light Up Princess Wand by Playmaker Toys)
- Lite Brite pegboard (sold by Hasbro) is a lighted board or box with small pegs to push into its frame. This is appropriate for older children who no longer put objects in their mouths.

LIGHTING CONSIDERATIONS

Ironically, although children with ASD love lights, they may be highly sensitive to overhead fluorescent lighting. Fluorescent lights send out pulsating vibrations that most people are unaware of but children with ASD may find very disturbing. One researcher found that fluorescent lights increased repetitive behavior in some children on the spectrum.[19] Adaptations include using natural lighting, using floor or desk lamps that shine directly onto the task, and wearing tinted glasses or a visor. These children may have what is called **scotopic sensitivity,** which is discussed at the end of this chapter.

Many children—typically developing or with ASD—are highly attracted to visual applications on electronic devices. There are specific apps designed to promote visual skills such as fixation and tracking, which I will discuss in Part II.

PROMOTING EYE CONTACT

For children on the autism spectrum, eye contact may be uncomfortable and distracting. Most people however interpret lack of eye contact as rude, or a sign of distrust or lack of interest. For this reason, it is beneficial for children with ASD to learn to look toward a speaker, perhaps by looking at the bridge of the person's nose, rather than directly into the eyes.

Try this game with a small group: Each child places a sticker between his or her eyebrows. Children take turns saying another child's name and what sticker that child is wearing. This is great to play at the beginning of the school year or at a new play group to help children learn each other's names.

ADDRESSING VISUAL DISTRACTIBILITY

Many children attend best in a low-stimulation environment, perhaps with bare walls and closed bins or covered shelves. I have found that many children with learning challenges do better when working with materials positioned directly in front of their eyes rather than on a table. Ways to accomplish this include standing at a whiteboard to write, placing materials on an easel or bookstand, or engaging in activities that are at eye level as shown photo 27.

27. Engaging in play or work at eye level promotes visual attention.

Reading Guides

Children who struggle with visual distraction may benefit from using a **reading guide** as shown in photo 28. This tool focuses them on a small viewing area as they move it across a page. Commercially available reading guides come with plastic windows that vary in size and color. Explore which color and size of window works best for your child. You can also make a reading guide by cutting a window in a strip of paper or card stock.

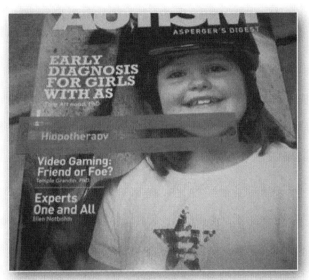

28. A reading guide with a tinted window helps a reader focus on a small area.

Promoting Visual Accommodation

Visual accommodation is the ability to keep the eyes in focus while shifting one's gaze between objects located at different distances or on different planes. For example, while driving most of us can glance down quickly at the speedometer then back at the road, naturally adjusting our eyes to see clearly at both distances. Children with poor accommodation skills may find it difficult to look back and forth between a black board in the distance and paper on the desk while copying information. The following activities may be helpful in developing this skill.

Adapted Puzzle (for Preschoolers)

This puzzle requires children to alternate between looking in the vertical and horizontal planes as they remove the puzzle pieces and insert them in the puzzle frame as shown in photo 29. It is made by placing the puzzle board in the bottom of a pizza box and attaching the puzzle pieces to the lid with Velcro hook-and-loop fastening.

29. An adapted puzzle is easily made from a pizza box.

Sequencing Pictures or Words (for Grade Schoolers)

Attach a row of pictures or playing cards to a vertical surface, such as a wall. Provide an identical set of cards on a desk or table. Have the child re-create the row on the wall using the cards on the table. Doing so requires alternating one's gaze between vertical and horizontal planes while arranging the cards in the same sequence (see photo 30). Start with only three or four cards and increase the number as the child gains skill. You can modify the activity by using cards with words, phrases, or sentences written on them. Increase challenge by spacing the cards on the vertical surface farther apart or farther from the child or both.

30. This sequence-matching activity requires looking
back and forth between two planes.

VISUAL PERCEPTION AND AUTISM

You previously learned that some individuals with ASD, including Temple Grandin, have amazing visual perceptual abilities. Grandin describes herself as "thinking in pictures" and says that using words is like a second language to her.[20] However, although people with ASD are often able to visualize and remember complex images, their visual abilities may be limited by a condition called **scotopic sensitivity, or Irlen syndrome.**[21] This is a visual perceptual problem that people with autism, learning disabilities, and related disorders may experience.

Scotopic sensitivity is an oversensitivity to bright lights, sunlight, glare, and fluorescent lights. Parents may notice that their child's behavior changes when they enter a supermarket, with an abrupt and overwhelming change in lighting. The lights may actually be painful! Other possible symptoms of scotopic sensitivity are

* Letters on a page may appear to jiggle.
* High-contrast materials may be difficult to interpret, such as headlights in the dark or black print on shiny white paper.
* The visual field may be restricted.
* Eye strain is common.
* Depth perception is impaired.

The Irlen lens system, created by educator Helen Irlen, uses tinted and colored lenses to reduce glare and contrast. The system may also use overlays or transparencies to improve reading. It is based on the theory that colors help make the world appear more three-dimensional, improving depth perception.[22] These products can only be obtained by visiting a practitioner trained in the Irlen system of assessment and treatment. Research on the Irlen lens system, like vision therapy in general, is limited.[23] Therefore, there is at present little scientific evidence to back up these claims.

SUMMARY: FUNCTIONAL VISION, VISUAL PERCEPTION AND HAND SKILLS

I. Functional vision refers to how a person uses eyesight to perform everyday tasks such as stacking blocks, dealing cards, or reading.

II. Some children have good visual perceptual abilities but challenges with functional vision.

III. Vision-related behaviors associated with ASD include poor eye contact; staring intently at spinning objects or lights; viewing objects out of the corner of the eye; and looking at an object, then looking away before picking it up.

IV. Optometrists are trained to prescribe eyeglasses or contact lenses to improve visual acuity.

V. Developmental optometrists specialize in diagnosing and treating disorders affecting functional vision.

VI. Developmental optometrists may recommend treatments such as prism glasses, color filters, patching the stronger eye to make the weaker eye work, vision therapy exercises, referral to an ophthalmologist, or referral to an OT for evaluation and possible treatment of a sensory processing disorder.

VII. Intervention strategies for babies involve use of visually stimulating toys such as tracking tubes. Activities for toddlers and preschoolers may include lights and multisensory toys, games, and activities.

VIII. It is beneficial for children with ASD to learn to look toward a speaker's eyes, or between the eyebrows, because the speaker may interpret a lack of eye contact as rude or a sign of distrust or disinterest.

IX. Possible strategies to address visual challenges include raising or angling materials, reading guides, visual accommodation activities, avoidance of florescent lighting, and use of scotopic lenses.

CHAPTER 4

Executive Functioning and Hand Skills

● ● ●

THE TERM EXECUTIVE FUNCTIONING MAY sound like it relates to financial management. However, neuroscientists use the term to refer to "the brain-based skills that are required for humans to execute, or perform, tasks."[24] Busy parents use their executive functioning to organize car pools and set priorities to meet their work and home schedules. Eight-year-old Alex uses executive functioning to put his toys away when his parents tell him to pick them up. His efficient executive functioning allows him to

Avoid distractions: to do the task even though the neighbor's kids are out playing

Problem solve: to avoid mixing his muddy outdoor toys together with his books

Make choices: ask Dad to help him move a heavy basketball stand rather than trying to do so by himself

Sustain his attention: to stay with the job until he completes it

Focus: to notice that his bicycle is lying in the street

Manage his time: to leave enough time to eat dinner and do his homework

Control his impulses: to clean up even though he'd rather play

I have worked with many children, including my son, who have not only found it very challenging to clean up, but have spent many stressful hours late into the night completing school assignments. A child's executive functioning affects every task throughout the day—whether it be remembering to close the bathroom door, finishing a spelling test before the bell rings, or deciding to get a different pair of socks when unable to find a match.

THE CHALLENGE OF GETTING THINGS DONE!

Dr. Jean Ayres describes autistic children as having difficulties with the "I want to do it" function in the brain. This function works closely with the sensory system that registers sensations and controls paying attention. These children may be able to plan and perform simple movements, such as lining up cars, but more complex actions do not occur to them. Children who have difficulty generating ideas tend to engage in stereotypic actions instead of the fluent, easy, quick, and imaginative motor actions typically developing children use in play.[25] The inner drive to plan and learn new actions is impaired in these children. Therefore, intervention strategies should include sensory stimulation that helps them to learn more complex motor skills that they can generalize to other situations.

Six-year-old Mary liked to repeatedly squeeze and release the adapted loop scissors in the air, oblivious to her classmates' annoyed looks. She noticed that all the other children in her first-grade class could cut out shapes, yet when she tried to control the scissors the paper ripped. She hated failure, so she refused to even touch the paper her teacher offered. During story time, Mary sprawled out over her mat, leaning her head on her hand. At other times she roamed aimlessly around the room, talking continuously about her dog, Ringo. When the teaching assistant tried to redirect her back to the mat, she began crying.

Mary waited to find her lunchbox until all the other children had taken theirs and were lined up by the door. She spent so much time in the lunchroom talking about what she was going to eat and finding someone to unzip her lunchbox for her that she seldom finished her entire lunch before the recess bell rang. Mary returned to class frustrated, hungry, and emotionally fragile.

Compared with her peers, Mary did have fine motor challenges. But several other difficulties also contributed to her delayed hand skills, specifically

Distractibility: She had difficulty maintaining attention long enough to perform a task.

Working memory: She could not remember how to unzip the lunchbox, so had to relearn this skill every lunchtime.

Emotional control: She became frustrated easily and would get so upset she could not focus on learning the more complex task of cutting paper.

Sustained attention: She had difficulty persisting with tasks long enough to practice or complete them.

Task initiation, planning, organization, and time management: She needs all these high-level skills to complete tasks in a reasonable time frame.

Flexibility and problem solving: Mary didn't make the connection that excessive talking and wandering prevented her from finishing her lunch.

When Mary was younger she didn't open and close her fingers, pretending to snip, the way her siblings had. Although she loved placing shapes into form boards, she never generalized that skill to placing stickers inside their corresponding outlines in a sticker book.

INTERVENTION STRATEGIES FOR MARY

Mary was diagnosed with ASD, ADHD, SPD, and a learning disability. She also had above-average intelligence. Lucy, the school OT, gave Mary small tongs to practice the open-and-close movements used for cutting with scissors. In addition, the teacher prepared a visual schedule with pictures showing the sequence of daily activities. Mary was allowed to go to the lunchroom ahead of the class so that she had extra time to eat, and her classroom aide helped her to choose a quiet place to sit. At Lucy's suggestion, Mary's mom bought her a new lunchbox with Velcro hook-and-loop closures so that she could set up and clean up her lunch without help.

> *Mary wanted to move and talk almost constantly. In response, Lucy created a sensory diet containing lots of structured deep pressure movement experiences that involved following directions. Mary had to finish an activity before she could speak. For example, Mary sat on the stationary platform swing and used tongs to pick up small dog biscuits and drop them into a box. Lucy pushed the swing slightly each time Mary dropped a biscuit into the box. After dropping in 10 biscuits, Mary's reinforcement was extra big, fast swinging while shouting out her favorite things to eat. The movement provided sensory stimulation while also encouraging Mary to persist at this task until completion. Mary was also rewarded with biscuits to take home to her dog, Ringo.*

Lucy used an eclectic approach to address Mary's executive functioning and sensory processing challenges, including a sensory diet, specific skill training (manipulating tongs), and reinforcement in the forms of movement and opportunities to shout.

Strategies for Executive Functioning Challenges

Some children talk all the time! They use talking to distract themselves and avoid challenges and possible failure. Many parents also love to talk so hesitate to tell their child to be quiet. However, children like Mary may not be able to plan and execute daily tasks if they are distracted by talking. Thus, they may not finish breakfast in time to catch the school bus.

Parents and teachers can easily become frustrated with children who have difficulty getting things done. Sometimes they may seem to be deliberately disobedient. However, children with executive functioning challenges need adults to create external structure for them as they gradually develop self-control. Here are some ways to do this.

TIMERS

There are many different types of auditory or visual timers (see the Resources) that can be used to make the passage of time concrete. Timers help children learn the expectations to complete specific tasks within reasonable time frames. For example, parents can teach their children that they must finish brushing their teeth within five minutes. If they finish sooner, there will be time to talk before the bus comes.

VISUAL SCHEDULES

A visual schedule is a sequence of pictures or words representing tasks the child needs to do. It can be as simple as a numbered list or set of pictures such as the following:

1. eat breakfast
2. put dirty dishes in sink
3. brush teeth
4. put on jacket
5. put on backpack

If my son David is spending too long eating breakfast or talking to me, I can point to or tap the picture of dirty dishes in the sink instead of discussing it. This strategy can be quite effective because visual skills are commonly a strength for children with ASD. This approach also avoids arguments!

Another type of visual schedule can be made by attaching pictures to a piece of cardboard with Velcro. Using detachable pictures enables the child to be involved in planning a schedule for a specific day- such as going to the playground followed by grocery shopping. Parents may also create a board divided into the categories of "Tasks to Do" and "Tasks Completed." Moving a picture from the first to second category creates a sense of accomplishment. The child can also see that a non-desired task (such as putting toys away) will be followed by a preferred task (such as reading a book in bed).

Preparation for Transitions

Children with executive functioning challenges need time to prepare for changes. Timers and visual schedules are two tools that help children make transitions. Parents can also use the verbal countdown technique, like this:

* We are leaving the park in 15 minutes.
* You can play another 10 minutes.
* OK, only 5 more minutes until we leave…

Giving Effective Directions

Make directions concrete and brief. You can use gestures with or in place of words. For example, say "use soap" or point to the soap to indicate that the child should use it. Mime washing your hands.

Break tasks into small steps and give prompts to persist until the entire task is completed:

1. Put all the plates in the dishwasher.
2. Now open the top rack.
3. Put the cups there.
4. Add soap.
5. Turn on the dishwasher.

Parents, teachers, and therapists strive to help children with executive functioning challenges develop the internal control they need to become more independent. For some children and adults, their goal may be to wash and dress themselves. Others need help and structure to complete school assignments, apply to college, or prepare for a work setting.

Summary: Executive Functioning and Hand Skills

 I. People use executive functioning skills to plan, execute, and remember motor tasks.

 II. Children with executive functioning weaknesses have challenges controlling the "I want to do it" function in the brain.

 III. Children with executive functioning challenges may have difficulties with focusing on the task at hand, problem solving, making choices, managing time, showing emotional flexibility, and controlling their impulses.

 IV. Children may engage in repetitive behaviors, such as opening and closing scissors in the air, because they have difficulty generating new ideas and planning their actions for more complex play.

 V. Children with executive functioning challenges need adults to create structure for them. Adding structure often helps these children succeed.

 VI. Adults can help provide this structure with use of timers, visual schedules, preparation for transitions, and effective modes of giving directions.

 VII. Children with executive functioning difficulties often benefit from a varied approach. This may include a sensory diet, skill-based training, and behavioral reinforcement.

CHAPTER 5

Using Reinforcement to Build Hand Skills

• • •

A BASIC PRINCIPLE IN SHAPING behaviors is that people want to repeat an action that leads to a desirable outcome. This is commonly referred to as a **positive consequence**. Mary, whom you met in the last chapter, was motivated to use tongs because she liked swinging. Swinging was the positive consequence that followed using the tongs. Therefore, she repeated the tongs activity in order to continue swinging. In this situation, movement functioned as a positive **reinforcer**. A reinforcer is a reward or an event that increases the likelihood of a behavior occurring. Reinforcement is best used to encourage positive behaviors. But sometimes adults also reinforce negative behaviors without realizing it. An example is when a child learns that he will get a candy bar every time he screams. Undesirable behaviors often decrease if they are ignored. Used carefully, reinforcement can be very effective.

Parents may use these principles when giving praise and dessert to the child who tries out a new vegetable but not to the child who refuses to eat any dinner. Note that praise and dessert only function as reinforcers if the child *likes* praise and dessert. Every child is an individual, so what is rewarding for one child may be meaningless, or even a negative consequence, for another. For example, parents usually think of "time-out" as a negative consequence. But for a child with SPD, time-out could be enjoyable because it offers a few minutes of "down time" when the child is getting overwhelmed. Similarly, a child who does not respond to words and avoids physical contact may find a hug and "I love you" an undesirable experience.

Here are reinforcers that many children may like:

* stickers
* video or computer game time
* time with a favorite person
* a preferred food
* hand lotion
* a whiff of perfume
* one minute of being left alone—for the child who needs a break after working hard
* playing on a swing, trampoline, merry-go-round, slide, or other movement equipment

Intensive behavioral interventions for children with ASD have been well researched and shown to be effective in teaching language, cognitive, self-care, and play skills.[26] These interventions are "intensive" because they are provided several hours daily, perhaps by parents or by professionals working in the home or school. One commonly used intervention is called Applied Behavior Analysis (ABA). For many children with ASD, interventions that involve sensory-based reinforcers may be effective in promoting hand use.

The Movement-Learning Link

Like all animals, humans are programmed to respond to movement in the environment. Knowing when to freeze like a statue helps a child to avoid detection during a game of hide-and-seek. Humans acclimate to movement. For example, after a few minutes in the car we lose awareness of speed and startle when the driver slams on the brakes. A toddler in a swing notices when the movement slows down and anticipates hearing the words "all done."

For most of us, movement is a joyful and natural part of life that never loses its appeal nor fills up the belly. Non-food reinforcers, such as movement, are desirable because they don't pose risks of choking, allergic reactions, or running out of snacks.

Movement also makes the human brain work better. When we move, more oxygen goes to the brain and we generally feel better. In fact, some people work at computers set up on treadmills. As I write this book, I alternate between using kneeling and ball chairs and taking walks around the block.

Movement—A Powerful Sensory Reinforcer

Movement can be a powerful reinforcer, because most children with ASD *love* to move! For example, during hippotherapy I use movement to reinforce communication: I might allow the horse to walk only after children say "go," sign "more," or point.

Fortunately, even without a horse, it is always possible to bring movement into an activity or use it as a reward for completing a task. Suspended swings, mini-trampolines, or other devices can provide intense movement. Even if you don't have this equipment, you can always have your child

* alternate touching toes and sky
* jump, hop, gallop, and skip
* do jumping jacks
* roll up inside a blanket or roll down a hill
* turn in circles
* dance

A child becomes alert when sensations from movement begin, stop, or change in direction or intensity. We can use this brief state of transition to promote engagement and hand use. For example, after running in place to music, a child might be especially engaged. He might then be willing to lie on his back while air "painting" letters or numbers on the ceiling. Let's take a look at how movement transitions can be used to reinforce hand use.

Three-year-old Billy typically arrives for his hippotherapy session flapping his hands and singing "Old McDonald." The singing seems to help Billy self-regulate—that is, stay calm—and at the same time avoid demands. He does not look at me but enjoys my greeting him with a bear hug. Billy ignores me as I help him mount the pony; when his hands touch anything—including the riding pad, reins, or pony's mane—he whines. Billy also does not appear to recognize the familiar volunteers as one leads the horse and the other walks beside him.

I have observed that Billy, like many of the children I work with, is more engaged after he rides for five or ten minutes. Knowing that movement calms him, I don't ask him to do or say anything until he has settled into the session. After some time trotting and walking up and down hills, I begin singing, "If you're happy and you know it, pat the pony." Billy ignores me when I demonstrate "pat the pony," so I tell the person leading the horse to stop. I give Billy a gentle nudge at his shoulder, and he pats the pony. Then he says "go." The leader starts the horse moving again. This provides the reinforcement of movement in response to Billy's engagement, functional hand use, and communication that he wanted to move again. We repeat this sequence, as I make up new verses to the song: "If you're happy and you know it . . .

- *clap your hands."*
- *touch the tail."*
- *give me high five."*

At first, I choose actions that I can physically guide Billy to do because he has not yet started to imitate or follow verbal directions. He learns that if he ignores my request, the consequence is that the movement will stop. Thus, he is motivated to comply with my requests to keep the horse moving. In this situation, movement acts as a sensory reinforcement. I might make casual comments during our session, such as "good job" or "there's a tractor." But I only make requests that require a response from him if I know I can help him to respond by stopping the horse then moving his hands. In other words, I don't want Billy to learn that he can get away with tuning me out. At the end of the song, we trot the pony for a few minutes to reward his engagement.

In this situation the sensory stimulation and reinforcement is primarily from the pony's movement. However, I could include other types of activities that provide sensory experiences and build hand skills. For example, I can ask Billy to pull the reins to stop the horse, then give him a ring to place over a vibrating toy.

Movement on horseback is extraordinarily motivating and stimulating. Other types of movement can be used in a similar fashion. For example, I can stop a swing or rocking chair from moving until the child performs an action- such as popping bubbles, then resume movement. Many other examples are possible. The key is to find a movement the child enjoys so much he is motivated to use his hands in order to get it.

Using Deep Pressure to Reinforce Hand Use

Many children with ASD love deep pressure sensory stimulation, especially when combined with movement. If your child is one of them, this section is for you. A child may be more motivated to use her hands when movement is combined with deep pressure. Here are examples:

1. Wendy lies prone on a large ball and gently bounces while reaching to match spelling word cards placed on the floor.
2. Wendy scoots across the room while sitting on a scooter board to retrieve clothespins she will use to hang up doll clothes.
3. Wendy squeezes snap cubes together to spell words (see photo 31).

31. Each snap cube has a letter on it. Children
receive sensory stimulation as they spell words.

Sensory stimulation may be incorporated into an intervention activity-such as when using a ring stack that vibrates, provided as reinforcement after completing the task, or both. For example, you could give reinforcers such as hand lotion or scent bottles to smell after children finish putting away their toys. Some children may be motivated to persist at an activity that involves moving "sensory bottles" from the floor to a tall box. Sensory bottles are a type of homemade "snow globe" filled with water, oil, glitter, and food coloring. They can be heavy and noisy and moving these bottles from low to high provides visual, auditory, proprioceptive and vestibular stimulation. Adapting activities to provide sensory stimulation or sensory-based reinforcement can be especially helpful when teaching children with limited functional hand use.

SUMMARY: USING REINFORCEMENT TO BUILD HAND SKILLS

    I. A reinforcer, or reward, is the desired consequence that makes a person want to repeat an action.

    II. Applied Behavioral Analysis (ABA) is an intervention that focuses on giving positive reinforcements or rewards so that a behavior is likely to be repeated.

    III. Reinforcers that provide sensory stimulation are especially powerful because they help meet the child's sensory needs

    IV. Many children with ASD love to move, so movement can be a very effective reinforcer.

    V. The nervous system becomes more alert when movement begins, stops, or changes in direction or intensity.

    VI. Other possible sensory-based rewards are providing scents; applying lotion; turning on flashing lights; shaking "sensory bottles"; or holding objects that vibrate or can be squeezed, pulled, or pushed.

    VII. Since each child is unique, parents and therapists must find what things or activities are rewarding for an individual child.

Part II

Interventions

● ● ●

CHAPTER 6

Teaching Strategies

● ● ●

THE MOST EFFECTIVE TEACHING STRATEGIES are individualized to meet the needs of the learner. This is true for anyone, old or young, with or without a disability, and regardless of cognitive ability. However, there are some general teaching principles that can help you begin finding the approaches that work best for your child or a student with ASD. You have previously learned several strategies to promote hand skills:

- Use movement or other sensory stimulation to reinforce behaviors; for example, allow jumping time after cleaning up art materials.
- Create an environment that supports visual needs through removing fluorescent lighting or using reading guides or other aids.
- Experiment with different seating options, weighted materials, and fidget tools.
- Provide executive functioning supports such as a picture or written schedule.
- Use repetition to develop and practice skills.

These general teaching strategies often benefit children in a small home school or resource room group or a larger classroom without a conspicuous adaptation that singles out the child with special needs as different. Let's look at a few more teaching strategies that may be especially helpful for children with ASD.

1. Use a cognitive approach to promote self-regulation.
2. Introduce small, gradual changes or challenges.
3. Teach "take-apart" before "put-together."
4. Use the 80-20 rule.
5. Don't be afraid of nonverbal directions.
6. Create success-only activities.
7. Find the best times to teach.
8. Break tasks down into steps.

COGNITIVE APPROACH FOR SELF-REGULATION

The Alert Program, created by occupational therapists Mary Sue Williams and Sherry Shellenberger, teaches children to use an engine as a metaphor for the brain.[27] Children choose activities that help their "engines" to run not too high, not too low, but just right. For example, if their "engine" is running too high, they may learn to lower it by choosing an activity such as rocking on a glider chair. Children who identify their engine as running "low" may choose to do jumping jacks to become more alert.

The ALERT Program uses both sensory- and cognitive-based strategies. Children don't need to understand the term "self-regulation," but they must have a self-awareness of how they feel and understand metaphors for how the brain is running (that is, fast or slow, high or low). The Alert Program was initially intended for children between ages 8 and 12, although it can be adapted for children who are chronologically or developmentally younger.[28]

A visual scale like the one shown in photograph 32 can help children to identify their current alertness level. Just draw a simple scale on paper or an erasable surface such as a whiteboard. They can write their names, or attach their names or photographs using Velcro or sticky notes, at the point on the scale that corresponds with their alertness. The goal is to move their names closer to the "Just Right" marking in the center by using activities that raise or lower their state of alertness. You could also illustrate this concept with a graphic such as a speedometer or a chart with slow and fast animals, ranging from a snail to a cheetah.

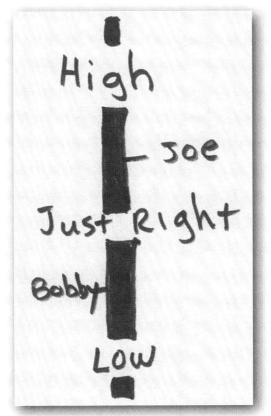

32. Students can use calming or alerting activities to bring themselves to a "Just Right" state.

SMALL, GRADUAL CHANGES OR CHALLENGES

Children with ASD typically do not like change. However, since the world is constantly changing, it is important to help children develop flexibility to cope. A good strategy is to introduce changes slowly and gradually. Here are a few examples:

* *Three-year-old John is willing to toss beanbags only with his right hand. His father made a few heavier "beanbags" from socks filled with sand. He gradually increased the weight until John had to use both hands to pick them up.*

* *Four-year-old Julia enjoys playing catch with a big plastic bag filled with packing peanuts. She avoids touching fabric, especially fur, wool, or anything with buttons or strings attached. Her occupational therapist attached some small pieces of fabric to the plastic bag. At first Julia refused to touch the "new bad bag" but then agreed to play while sitting on a vibrating cushion. Gradually, Julia learned to tolerate balls with various textures in her game of catch.*

* *Six-year-old Patricia will work on art projects only when she is alone with her classroom aide. The teacher placed a volunteer student nearby. This new student worked quietly and independently. Eventually, Patricia accepted having this student sit at her table and share crayons.*

* *Ten-year-old Ernie refuses to eat in the cafeteria. He is, however, willing to sit right outside the door at a table set up for him, if he wears headphones. Ernie has learned to tolerate removing the headphones for the last five minutes of lunchtime while the teacher reads a story to him. Eventually, he tolerates having another child join him.*

TEACH TAKE-APART BEFORE PUT-TOGETHER

Have you noticed that it is easier to open or remove objects than to close or attach them? I have found this true when I teach children to open knots, clothing fasteners, screw caps, and lids. It is also easier to remove the contents from a bag or envelope than to fill it. So I teach children how to manipulate objects by opening or removing before closing or attaching!

A "take-apart box" is a wonderful way to teach children how to unscrew caps. The one shown in photo 33 is made by cutting holes in a box, then pushing threaded pieces cut from juice cartons through the holes. Use tape to secure the threaded pieces in place.

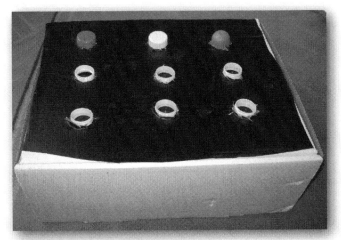

33. Children practice unscrewing the caps from this "take-apart box."

This adaptation enables children to practice a skill repeatedly, and you can choose the size and number of caps to use according to your child's abilities. The larger screw-on covers shown in photo 34 were cut from detergent, juice, and dishwasher soap bottles. After children learn how to unscrew caps, teach the more challenging skill of screwing them back on.

34. These covers and threaded pieces can be used in "take-apart boxes."

Try to encourage visual attention by angling or raising the "take-apart box" using a bookstand. An alternative is to attach the threaded pieces to all four sides of a large cardboard box with the top removed. Then children can drop the caps inside after unscrewing them. Here are a few other "undoing" tasks that may be easier to learn before the "doing" task:

* Pulling off socks and removing other clothing is easier than dressing.
* Unscrewing nuts and bolts is easier than connecting them.
* Removing paper fasteners, clips, or squeeze pins from paper is easier than attaching them.

THE 80-20 RULE

The "80-20 rule" used in the field of education is based on the principle of avoiding or limiting failure. It says to give children 80% work that they have already learned before introducing 20% that is new or challenging.[29] Spending time on known material or experiences enables children to practice and reinforce skills while building their confidence. I suggest following up attempts to do the 20% challenging tasks with some much-desired sensory reinforcement! Of course, you might bend this rule one direction or another based on your child's needs. But the basic principle is that a child should experience success much more often than failure. The 80-20 rule may also limit or prevent agitation. As you can see, this principle can also be applied to promote social success.

When my son David was a 12-year-old boy scout he loved to go camping with his troop. However, he was easily overwhelmed by the demands of interacting with a group of energetic boys while pitching tents, preparing food, and making a fire. Leo, the scout leader, recognized that David needed to spend a good hour gathering wood by himself before interacting with the other boys to build a fire. Leo praised David for creating a woodpile (the easy 80%) and then paired him up with another scout to start building the fire (the challenging 20%). Gathering wood gave David lots of heavy pressure sensory stimulation that helped him to relax and prepare to interact socially with his peer. The entire troop was rewarded with a blazing fire and hot meal.

Nonverbal Directions

You learned in chapter four how to make directions concrete and brief. It is also important to understand that many individuals with ASD tune out verbal directions entirely or simply repeat the last word they heard, regardless of the communicative intent. Nonverbal directions can help children who tend to ignore words. Try pointing to, looking at what needs to be done, or giving an auditory cue. For example, I could point to or tap the faucet to communicate "turn on the water." I may look at a coat hook and clear my throat until the child holding his coat realizes that he needs to hang it up. Touching a child's writing hand may him to focus on a writing task. Use trial and error to see what works best with your child.

Success-Only Adaptations

Another helpful strategy is to adapt activities for "success only." This means the activity will work only if done correctly. The bottle shown in photograph 35 teaches how to discriminate pennies from quarters and nickels. Only pennies fit through the slot in the bottle; the quarters and nickels are too large, and there are no dimes.

Assist the child to find the brown pennies to insert. This is a great way to help impulsive children slow down to examine size and color. In addition, many children with ASD prefer nonverbal feedback to verbal correction. Success-only activities do just that. This is one reason most children with ASD love computers and apps that reward them repeatedly but only when they perform a task correctly. Here are other examples:

* Cut and remove a circle from a sheet of thick paper; then tape the sheet on top of another sheet of paper. Have the child color

35. Failure is impossible, because only the pennies
fit through the slot in this bottle.

over the hole in the top sheet. When the top sheet is removed, the
bottom sheet will reveal a perfectly colored circle below. The top
sheet functions as a disposable stencil.

* Here's a way to teach your child how to fill a container without
dumping out the contents. Tape a magnet to the bottom of a tall
container, then let the child drop magnetic objects inside. The
objects won't fall out if she turns the container over before com-
pletely filling it up. Simply untape the magnets when it is time to
empty the container.

* Ask a child to count out a certain number of objects and place
them in container sections that correspond to that number. For
example, tell your child to count out 12 plastic eggs from a bowl
that holds many more, placing each one in an egg carton slot. The
child will only be able to count out 12 before filling the carton.

The Best Times to Teach Skills

Teach a new skill when the child has plenty of time to process directions and practice it. Bear in mind that many children learn best in the morning or after a snack or movement break. Consider when your individual child is most motivated to learn or perform a skill. For example, some children would be very motivated to help tie their shoes before going out to play; others would be too excited to focus. Perhaps the best time to practice dressing oneself is after a relaxing bath.

Step-by-Step Tasks

When we break down a complex task into steps, we can see which steps are easier versus more difficult to perform. For example, it is easier to pull the tab on a connected zipper than to connect the two halves. **Backward chaining** involves teaching the last step first. It works well when the last step is the easiest. Then the child can take pride in completing a task that someone else started—such as raising the zipper once the halves are connected. Once the child learns how to pull up the zipper, she can tackle the more challenging task of joining the two halves.

Forward chaining is the opposite of backward chaining. This technique is useful when the first step in a sequence is the easiest. For example, putting a helmet on one's head is a lot easier than buckling it.

Some children learn best when given **hand-over-hand assistance (HOH)**. In this technique, the instructor places his/her hands over the child's hands. By guiding the child's hand movements the instructor helps the child experience what the motions feel like. For example, HOH assistance to pour juice from a pitcher allows a child to experience the sensations of

* lifting the pitcher
* moving it to touch the glass
* tilting it to pour

Over time, the instructor can offer less guidance, allowing the learner to participate more. Hand-over-hand training sends the message that although the child does not yet have the skill, he can be involved to the extent possible. Children with tactile defensiveness may not tolerate HOH training, or they may tolerate it better when combined with sensory-based strategies. Try having the child wear a weighted vest or warming up the child's hand with deep pressure massage.

Your child may benefit from one or several of the teaching strategies described in this section— and the ones that work best will change as your child gets older. Only trial and error—and time—will tell.

Summary: Teaching Strategies

I. A cognitive approach to self-regulation requires the child to understand complex concepts—such as an engine as a metaphor for the brain.

II. Children with ASD typically do not like change. Changes and challenges should be gradual and small.

III. Taking something apart (or off) is generally easier than putting it together (or on). Start with the easier task first.

IV. The 80-20 rule means that a learner should engage in previously learned and successful activities for a large amount of time, followed by a small amount of time on new or challenging activities.

V. Some children follow nonverbal directions better than verbal ones. For example, pointing to napkin may be more effective than saying, "Wipe your face."

VI. Success-only activities provide immediate, nonverbal clues about whether the child is doing the activity correctly.

VII. Identify the times or situations when your child learns best. Introduce new activities at those times.

VIII. Breaking down complex tasks into steps enables a child to learn the easiest steps first. Forward and backward chaining are two teaching options.

IX. Backward chaining involves teaching the last step in a sequence—first. This may be effective when the last step is relatively easy.

X. Forward chaining involves teaching the first step of a sequence—first. This may be effective when the first step is relatively easy.

XI. In hand-over-hand (HOH) assistance, the instructor moves the learner's hands through the motions of a task so that the learner can experience how it feels.

CHAPTER 7

Apps as Teaching Tools

• • •

SWIPING, TAPPING, OR USING "DRAG and release" movements on a tablet or smartphone device require relatively less fine motor control than, say, connecting dots to form pictures or writing one's name. Electronic devices may help children to demonstrate visual perceptual skills, such as fitting puzzle pieces together or tapping on hidden pictures on a screen, without the fine motor challenge of connecting or circling them. For some people, an electronic device can give the life-changing ability to communicate for the first time.

> *At four years of age, Carly was nonverbal and frequently had outbursts where she would wail and slap the table. She had clear signs of intelligence— she pointed to pictures to identify what she wanted and could complete a 100-piece jigsaw puzzle faster than an adult could. It was hard to gauge her intellectual abilities though, because of her tantrums and hyperactivity. Her speech-language therapist thought that much of Carly's behavior stemmed from frustration over her difficulty communicating.*
>
> *Arthur Fleishman, Carly's father, describes in his book* Carly's Voice, *how, after several years of ABA and other therapies, his then 10-year-old daughter had learned to type words and short phrases on a device that functioned as a sophisticated picture book with voice output.*
>
> *She wasn't very interested in the alphabet function, and the thera- pists were planning to delete it to make room for more pictures and sym- bols. But on the fateful date of March 10, 2005, Carly was especially*

restless and crabby. She grabbed the device and tapped out H-E-L-P T-E-E-T-H H U-R-T. Her therapists and family were stunned. They had no idea she was capable of that level of communication. That day, Carly's voice was born.[30]

For the past two decades students with handwriting difficulties have benefited from portable word processors with word prediction programs that make typing faster, easier, and more accurate. Technology has enabled children with learning and physical disabilities to compensate for their limitations in a way similar to how eyeglasses help those with visual impairments. Children like Carly, growing up in the digital age, fit right in with all the tech-savvy kids who have smartphones glued to their ears and tablets in their backpacks. Typical adolescents might view their devices as essential for their social and entertainment needs. In contrast, parents of children with autism often recognize they are a lifeline to learning.

Do you remember "Touch and Tell Electronic Learning," a toy made by Texas Instruments in the early 1980s? It was a simple board covered with pictures. A robotic voice either named the picture that was pressed or gave a directive such as "Touch the red ball." My son loved this toy for many reasons:

- It allowed him to repeat an action that produced a predictable response as many times as he wanted.
- The voice was a robotic monotone; therefore, he did not need to understand inflections or facial expressions.
- The programmed sentence was short and concise.
- The voice immediately confirmed a correct or incorrect response with words such as—"You touched the ball" or "Try again."

Many apps on modern-day tablet or smartphone devices have the same basic characteristics. However, the range of learning opportunities and types of reinforcements has grown tremendously. IPads and other tablets are very popular today because they are large enough to type on comfortably yet small enough to pull out and use all day long. They are also less expensive than a desktop or laptop computer. The Apple company has pioneered a tremendous variety of interactive apps that help children with special needs to

- learn cognitive concepts, ranging from colors to counting to how to choose the right clothing for the weather conditions
- read, spell, pronounce words, and use proper grammar
- follow visual schedules
- communicate with pictures or icons
- type with word-prediction options
- develop fine motor skills, including handwriting

The sheer quantity of apps to choose from can be overwhelming. The book *Apps for Autism*, by speech-language pathologist Lois Jean Brady, is a very useful resource.[31] She did the work of reviewing the apps most relevant to the autism community—presenting pros and cons, prices, and manufacturers. Many of the apps she includes are designed to develop motor planning skills and teach the fundamental concept of **cause-and-effect relationship**.

LEARNING CAUSE AND EFFECT

At around 12 months of age, typically developing babies can control their index finger well enough to touch or press buttons on toys, remote controls, telephones, and other household objects. Through these actions babies learn that they can control their environment to make things happen. They are learning about cause-and-effect relationships. Younger babies use this knowledge when they deliberately shake a rattle to make a sound. Older babies enjoy cause-and-effect toys that require more difficult fine motor skills. They might pull a lever or rotate a dial to make something happen. Toddlers learn that squeezing a doll can make it squeak or the eyes pop out, and older children learn cognitive concepts such as color matching when a toy key only opens the lock on a door of the same color.

Many children with ASD avoid these types of toys because they lack the hand strength or coordination to make them work. These children may not only miss out on the type of play that builds hand skills, they have fewer opportunities to learn concepts such as mixing yellow and red paint to create orange or moving a crayon through a path in order to reach an endpoint. Electronic toys help children to learn such cause-and-effect concepts.

As I explained earlier, many children with ASD are motivated to use sensory toys that have, say, flashing lights or music. Tablets and smartphones also offer attention-grabbing animations and videos. Let's take a look at how a few apps utilize sensory stimulation to help children build fine motor skills.

Developing Fine Motor Control

Electronic devices may promote hand skills that are very simple—such as activating animal sounds by touching the screen with the whole hand (see *The Farm Animals*).[32] Others may require greater motor control, such as using an index finger to touch small pictures in order to activate sounds (see *I Hear Ewe*).[33] In both situations the child learns that visually attending to and touching pictures produce a desirable result. After children develop skills to touch stationary pictures, they can develop the eye-hand coordination to touch moving ones, such as the balloons in *Balloon Pops*.[34] The game *Falling Apples* develops bilateral hand use as the child tilts the electronic device to move a basket and catch falling apples.[35] Many apps help children develop the motor control to swipe, drag, and release in order to make things happen. For example *First Words Sampler* requires dragging and releasing letters to spell words that label a picture.[36]

Paper-and-pencil mazes can be frustrating for children who lack control to draw between the lines with a pencil or stylus. An app can make this task easier by enabling children to trace a path through a maze with a finger. In addition, many apps (such as *MazeFinger Plus*) have motivating sound and visual effects.[37] Apps that involve tracing lines and shapes help develop the motor control required to write letters using pencil and paper. Here are some IPad apps that teach letter formation:

Dexteria[38] consists of three games:

1. *Write-It:* Children trace inside letter outlines. A dot indicates where to begin forming the letter.
2. *Pinch-It:* Children pinch bugs to make them disappear. This develops coordination between the index finger and thumb.
3. *Tap-It:* Children tap lit-up circles—it's like playing the game *Twister* using the fingers! This is a great way to develop dexterity.

Letter School[39] also involves tracing letter and number outlines, but the visual effects and music are very fun and motivating. There are three skill levels for each letter and number:

1. The child just needs to touch where the letter begins; the app will complete the letter and produce music/visual effects.
2. The child must trace within the letter outline in the correct sequence and stay within the lines.
3. The child has a visual cue for where to start, but must form the letter without an outline.

Ready to Print[40] consists of 13 activities designed to teach specific fine motor skills, including how to

1. touch, drag, and release
2. trace inside mazes
3. trace shapes, letters, or numbers
4. connect dots to form shapes
5. use a pinching motion to bring items on the screen together
6. draw with fingers or use a stylus (a tool grasped like a pencil)

Electronic devices are no substitute for toys that children can manipulate in their hands. Children need to handle toys to learn about size, shape, weight, and other sensory qualities of objects. Electronic devices do, however, offer a learning alternative for children who may avoid using their hands due to sensory sensitivities or poor coordination. Games, puzzles, and other apps that require visual discrimination and good memory skills enable children with ASD to show off their strengths while doing something that they love.

SUMMARY: APPS AS TEACHING TOOLS

I. Computers, tablets, and smartphones are electronic devices that may help children with ASD develop hand skills.

II. Electronic toys offer repetition, predictability, immediate feedback, and experience with cause-and-effect relationships.

III. Apps may provide sensory reinforcement through sound and visual effects, including animation or videos.

IV. Apps may develop several fine motor skills, such as touching and dragging, swiping, pinching, tracing with an index finger, or controlling a stylus to form letters.

V. Electronic devices may be especially beneficial for children who have difficulties paying attention and avoid touching, or manipulating objects.

VI. Children with ASD often have strengths in the areas of visual discrimination and memory. Apps may showcase these strengths.

CHAPTER 8

Promoting Handwriting Skills

● ● ●

HANDWRITING IS ARGUABLY ONE OF the most difficult fine motor skills a
young child is required to learn. Not every child is developmentally ready
at ages five or six to sit in a chair without sliding down and pay attention
in a roomful of squirmy bodies that might be too close, too loud, and too
overwhelming, especially for a child who has ASD. Teachers frequently
refer kindergarteners and first-graders for occupational therapy evalu-
ations because they struggle with handwriting, but sometimes the best
strategy is simply to give children the time they need to mature. It may be
helpful for parents to understand the foundational skills, or **prewriting
skills,** that children should attain before being taught how to form letters
and numbers. Strategies that address these skills follow later in this chapter. Prewriting skills include abilities to

- sit with good postural control—not sliding out of the chair or resting the head on one hand
- effectively control a writing tool, such as a crayon, marker, paintbrush, or pencil
- understand concepts of directionality, size, and length, such as up
  and down, big and small, and tall and short. All are needed in
  order to form the letter *H* with two long vertical lines connected
  by one short horizontal line.
- differentiate similar shapes, such as diagonal lines slanting toward
  the left versus toward the right

- discriminate right and left on shapes in order to identify and form letters such as *d* and *b*.
- follow a sequence of pictures or words on a page from left to right and top to bottom
- form lines and shapes that make up letters. The vertical + and diagonal × crosses are the basis of letters formed with a combination of vertical and slanted lines, such as *V*, *N*, or *Y*

Children with ASD may miss out on important developmental experiences that prepare them for writing. Because of their sensory, motor, and social challenges they may currently avoid, or have avoided when they were younger, experiences of

- tummy time and crawling
- manipulating small toys with both hands
- visual tracking—for example, following a ball moving through the air or moving a finger through a maze
- forming lines and shapes in finger paint
- pretending to write—such as scribbling a shopping list

Some of the strategies described in earlier chapters may help children to develop certain prewriting skills.

HANDWRITING IS MORE THAN FORMING LETTERS AND NUMBERS

Children typically first learn to form very large letters and numbers on unlined paper. Given practice they develop the motor control to form smaller ones and eventually to fit them between lines. There are many different types of lined paper designed to help children form letters correctly. They usually have a solid **base line,** or **writing line.** Photograph 36 shows how the letters are oriented to sit on the bold base line.

36. Paper with a solid bold base/writing line indicates where letters should "sit".

Using lined paper can be quite challenging since children have to follow the rules of making letters fit in the correct spaces. The half-space letters *e, c, i,* and *n* fit between the base line and the broken line above it. Uppercase letters and lowercase **ascender letters** such as *R, h, k,* or *t* extend above the broken line. **Descender letters** such as *y* and *g* dip below the base line. Some children struggle with the following aspects of writing:

* Forming letters and numbers with correct sizing (They might make half-space letters, such as *e* and *i,* the same size as whole-space letters such as *R* and *l.)*
* Orienting letters and numbers to sit on the base line with the descender lines dipping below it.
* Creating uniform spaces between words.
* Using adequate pressure so that their writing can be seen but not pressing down so hard that the paper rips.
* Writing laboriously and taking excessive time to complete a task.

Children with these types of issues may be referred for an OT evaluation to determine what aspect of writing is difficult and what strategies may help them. One of these children is Gary, whom you met earlier. Gary has a learning disability as well as challenges with sensory processing, functional vision, and executive functioning.

Seven-year-old Gary is able to read out loud but reverses words (saying "nam" instead of "man"). He is able to copy words if given a model on the same piece of paper. But if he has to look back and forth between the board and paper, he makes many errors. Gary struggles to grasp the pencil in a way that allows him to see the lines he is forming. His letters are legible but are all the same size, and there are no spaces between words. His hands are weak and he has low muscle tone. Gary has learned that he can control the pencil better if he uses "the death grip." He holds the pencil so tightly that his knuckles turn white and his hand begins to ache after writing only a few words. When Gary's teacher asks him to do more, he runs away.

Older students with ASD have multiple challenges. First, it is difficult to write when struggling to attend; sit with good posture; stabilize the paper; and control the pencil to form letters and words with good sizing, spacing, and legibility. Second, these students often have difficulties generating ideas to put on paper. Authors Cheryl Boucher and Kathy Oehler remind us that "even simple writing tasks require skills in areas that are often very difficult for individuals with ASD: language, organization, sensory regulation, and motor control.[41]

STRATEGIES THAT PROMOTE WRITING

This chapter explores strategies that help children with ASD to use a pencil effectively to write. The Resources section lists books and websites to help children with writing challenges.

Let's begin by adding sensory fun to writing!

Five-year-old Doreit prefers to run around, but she is willing to work when sitting on a vibrating cushion. Her teacher provides the cushion only during prewriting time. That makes this practice "special." Doreit has learned to associate "writing time" with various special sensory treats, such as

- *aromas, incense, or scented markers*
- *a motorized pen that makes squiggly lines*
- *music that is played in the room or through headphones*
- *a weighted or squeeze vest*

POSITIONING PAPER

I mentioned previously that children may have better visual attention for materials positioned directly in front of their face, rather than on a table. The same is true when writing: encourage young children to color or write on a whiteboard, chalkboard, large easel, or paper taped to a wall. A slant board is also beneficial; vertical or angled writing surfaces place the wrist in the optimal position to control a pencil. You can buy a slant board (see the Resources) or make one by clipping paper to a large empty binder. The binder shown in photograph 37 has been covered with adhesive shelf paper, and a clip has been attached to secure the paper.

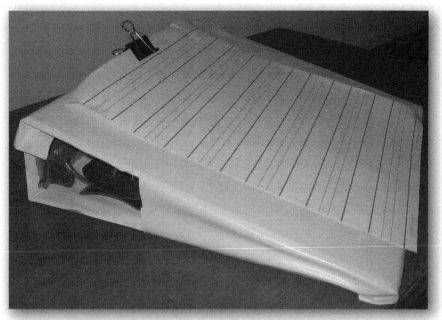

37. An empty binder made into a slant board for writing.

Although children can write using various pencil grasps, the **tripod grasp** is considered the most efficient for motor control and comfort. This grasp got its name because the middle finger, index finger, and thumb look like a tripod stand. Some children may write more comfortably using a large-sized pencil or a pencil with a rubber pencil grip that gives them a larger surface to grasp. (See the Resources for options.) To enlarge the gripping area, simply wrap a rubber band around a pencil about an inch above the point. Some pencils and pencil grips have indentations that indicate finger placement used in the tripod grasp.

Start Big!
Children may best learn how to form letters by copying the instructor's large arm movements to form giant letters in the air. This helps their muscles learn how the strokes feel and the correct sequence of movements. Remember Gary? He has poor body awareness and the following big movement activities help him to learn letter formation:

1. Imitating the teacher as she forms letters by moving her arm and hand in the air. The teacher stood with her back to the class so that they all had the same right-left orientation.
2. Forming shapes, letters, and numbers using chalk on the sidewalk, pieces of rug squares or sandpaper. Pressing down with chalk is very resistive, helping children to *feel* the movements used to form letters.
3. Tracing giant letters on a whiteboard.
4. Drawing inside large letters drawn with a highlighting marker on unlined paper

Children first have to learn to form letters proficiently. Only then can they orient the letters on a base or writing line, with appropriate sizing and spacing between letters and words.[42] Thus, children benefit from lots of free practice forming large letters on large, unlined surfaces.

Use a Multisensory Approach

Gary's teacher preferred to use a multisensory approach to enhance learning. Gary did many tasks that engaged his tactile, proprioceptive, and visual senses:

- completing lacing boards in the shapes of letters and numbers
- rolling clay snakes that he shaped into letters and numbers
- forming letters and numbers with pipe cleaners
- sorting shapes, letters, words, or numbers written on cards or objects. This activity enables the child to work on visual discrimination and manipulation skills at the same time (see photo 38).

Gary also enjoyed tracing letters on his IPad, especially when rewarded with music and animations.

38. These cards are designed to help children discriminate diagonal lines and shapes.

ORIENTING LETTERS TO LINED WRITING PAPER

Once Gary could form letters he was ready to use the following Velcro strip activity that teaches how to fit letters on guide lines with spaces between words.

Attach three strips of Velcro fastener to a frame. The frame shown in photo 39 is a large plastic envelope that also provides storage. Cut small ovals and circles out of white plastic milk bottles. The taller ovals are used to write uppercase and ascender and descender letters (such as *H*, *p*, *y* and *d*) and the smaller circular shapes are used to write half-space letters such as *a* or *s*. Attach dots of Velcro to the letter pieces so that they can be repeatedly rearranged on the board.

39. A Velcro frame helps teach letter placement.

Use dry-erase marker so that the shapes can be wiped clean and reused. Show children how to spell a word or short phrase, choosing the correct large or small shape to write letters on. They then place the letters on the Velcro fastener strips, in the correct order and position. This provides a visual and tactile experience as they feel and see how the letters relate spatially to one another.

ADAPTED PAPER

Commercially available graph or adapted writing paper can help children to size and orient letters. Adapted paper may have

* color coding to indicate where letters fit
* raised tactile ridges to indicate the base/writing line
* bold base or writing lines
* broken lines to show where half-space letters fit

Although adapted paper can be very helpful, I emphasize again that children should not be expected to have the motor control or visual perception to use lined paper appropriately until they have mastered forming letters and numbers on unlined paper. There are many games and activities—such as letter-forming app games, letter shaped sewing cards, letter tracing and connect the dots work sheets—that can be used to develop these skills.

SPACING TOOLS

A spacing tool can be as simple as an index finger or a wooden craft stick. The child places the stick or his finger on the paper at the end of a word to create a space before writing the next word. Cute commercially available spacing tools are sold in sizes to match the type of paper being used. You can also use graph paper to teach letter size and spacing. The child simply leaves an empty box between each word.

Please see the Resources for more information about adapted writing paper and spacing tools. For some children writing by hand will never be practical. Writing may be too slow, too frustrating, and illegible. These children are lucky to live in the digital age of computer and tablet app options. A team of parents, teachers, and therapists should discuss the best option for each individual child.

SUMMARY: PROMOTING HANDWRITING SKILLS

I. All children should master prewriting skills before being taught to form letters and numbers.

II. Prewriting skills include being able to
   * maintain a stable posture
   * control a pencil
   * distinguish and form shapes used to make letters and numbers
   * recognize right and left
   * move along lines on a page from left to right and top to bottom

III. Children should be proficient at forming letters and numbers before being expected to fit them on lined paper.

IV. Some children have difficulties with handwriting because they missed out on or avoided important early developmental experiences. These include tummy time, crawling, forming lines and shapes in finger paint, and manipulating small objects.

V. Children with ASD may have difficulties with the motor control, sensory processing, visual perceptual, and communication aspect of writing.

VI. Possible beneficial adaptations include special paper, pencil grips, vertical or angled writing surfaces, spacing tools, and multisensory teaching activities.

CHAPTER 9

Adults with Autism Spectrum Disorders

● ● ●

ADULTS WITH AUTISM HAVE UNIQUE sensory, motor, social, and communication abilities. Some of them will use technology to compensate for fine motor difficulties. Others—like Temple Grandin and my son—may use their excellent hand dexterity to achieve a high level of independence. Individuals with cognitive, motor, and behavioral challenges may move from special education programs into vocational training, sheltered workshops, or adult day programs to continue learning functional skills. Skill training objectives may focus on areas such as

- personal care, including hygiene, grooming and dressing skills-such as washing hands, shaving, and brushing hair
- daily living skills unrelated to personal care- such as managing laundry, using a telephone and preparing meals
- prevocational skills that prepare them for volunteer or paid work-such as using a photocopier, collating, stuffing envelopes, assembly tasks, or bagging school lunches.

Adult day programs often emphasize decreasing maladaptive behaviors, increasing quality of life, and helping individuals to be as independent as possible. Teaching academics is usually not a focus. Maladaptive behaviors are socially inappropriate actions—such as screaming or biting one's hand—that hinder a person from participating in the day-to-day world. The person with ASD may use these behaviors as a way to cope with sensory challenges. A good adult services program strives to meet the person's sensory needs in safe and acceptable ways, while creating social and communication opportunities throughout the day. A team of therapists—occupational therapist, physical therapist, speech-language pathologist, and behaviorist—may work together to design programs that

* promote health, safety, and cardiovascular fitness
* reduce agitation and promote calm
* expand leisure, prevocational or vocational options

In other words, day program should be designed to help adults with ASD to have the best quality of life possible. As an occupational therapist I try to use the adult's strengths and skills to create meaningful activities. For example, for people who have the cognitive ability to enjoy pictures, I may ask them to sort pictures of their peers. I may ask individuals who can read words to hang laminated printed phrases (with holes punched into them) onto a hook board. It is important to design activities that meet the individual's developmental and sensory needs without being childish. For example, one gentleman I work with enjoys folding laminated pictures of Civil War historical events in order to fit them into a container slot. He enjoys talking about the pictures, and this is more age and developmentally appropriate (given his cognitive abilities) than inserting bingo chips or pictures of Disney characters.

Many of the activities I have described in this book can be adapted for adults. For example, Clara is a young woman who enjoys removing heavy containers from a cart and placing them along the floor of the hallway. Clara likes saying "hi" to the people she passes. She tends to flap and at times bite her hands when bored or overstimulated. Pushing the cart and moving up and down to place the containers provides sensory stimulation that helps her to remain calm. This activity also practices sequencing skills similar to unloading books from a library cart or stocking store shelves.

Ira has difficulties with transitions, especially getting off the transportation van. He sometimes arrives at his program in an agitated state—mumbling under his breath and slapping his head. On these days he is eager to engage in the sensory activities that staff set up for him. These activities appear to help him calm down and meet his sensory needs. Ira enjoys

* *taking fast walks while carrying detergent bottles filled with sand*
* *filling his backpack with the weighted socks that are lined up along the hallway*
* *sitting at a table with objects to squeeze, press, and pull apart.*
* *perform the coil stringing activity shown in photo 40.*

Offering these types of sensory-based coping strategies usually prevent Ira's agitation from escalating into a tantrum that involves throwing objects. When Ira is calm enough he is able to enjoy eating a morning snack and playing games on an IPad.

40. Pulling the coil upward provides sensory stimulation.

The coil used in the stringing activity is cut from a watering hose. A bag of sand is tied onto the bottom of the coil. Ira stands on the bag to keep the coil in place while he places small rings on the top end he is pulling upward. I made the rings by cutting sections of plastic tubing. They are a bit smaller than the rings used to hang shower curtains. You could also cut flat doughnut shapes out of plastic.

Ira must use force to pull the coil upward so that the rings spiral down the coil. He enjoys the sensations his muscles and joints receive when pulling the coil upward and the visual stimulation of watching the rings twirl downward.

By the time adults enter a day program, they have already had years of special education services that included academic and functional skills training. At this point, it is important to decide which skills would be both beneficial and realistic for the individual to learn.

For example, 25 year-old Ira does not have the cognitive abilities to identify or sort coins. However, he enjoys picking out coins that are mixed into a box of checkers and inserting them into a piggy bank. Ira recognizes that manipulating money is an adult activity and that he is able to do this task successfully. The 80-20 rule works well for Ira. After spending a large amount of time independently filling the piggy bank, he is willing to spend a short amount of time on a more challenging skill. This involves picking out pennies from a pile of pennies and quarters to insert into a container slot. The slot is too small for the quarters to fit. Ira easily gets frustrated when given verbal directions but tolerates this type of success-only teaching strategy.

Sometimes a more effective teaching strategy can allow adults to succeed in learning skills that they previously attempted and failed to learn. For example, I have helped adults learn how to close buttons by practicing on large button squares, then progressively smaller ones. Eventually, they were able to button their own clothing, giving them a new level of independence.

Many young adults with ASD who have average or above average cognitive abilities are happier once they can spend time doing and studying what they enjoy and are good at, rather than what the school curriculum requires. My son found his quality of life improved when he could focus on math and science. In an ideal world people like him would be allowed to create work environments that support their sensory needs. An accommodating workplace may allow employees to

* work at a standing or treadmill desk
* hold walking meetings
* wear headphones to block out noise or listen to calming music
* chew gum

This type of flexibility might create a more productive work environment for everyone, not just people on the autism spectrum.

SUMMARY: ADULTS WITH AUTISM SPECTRUM DISORDERS

    I. Adult programs typically shift away from a focus on academics to teaching functional skills.

   II. Functional skills include training in the areas of self-care, daily living skills, and prevocational skills.

  III. Many of the strategies described throughout this book can be adapted for adults.

  IV. Activities should be age-appropriate and designed to utilize the adult's strengths—such as reading and writing.

    V. Sometimes using different teaching strategies will enable adults to master skills they were previously unable to learn.

  VI. Adaptations or accommodations in work environments may help adults with ASD to succeed in higher education and a career.

A Few Closing Thoughts

● ● ●

I BEGAN THIS BOOK BY introducing you to Gary. This young boy would immediately catch your eye because he used his hands in atypical ways. Like many children with ASD, Gary's hand skills were limited by difficulties with sensory processing, functional vision, and executive functioning. He spent hours flapping his hands and lining up objects. Although the diagnostic criteria for ASD center on social, communication, and repetitive behaviors, hand skills also reflect the challenges children with ASD face.

I wrote this book to share how those of us who work with and love children can detect and address the earliest red flags of visual, sensory, and motor impairments. We can address these issues early, perhaps even before a child receives a diagnosis of ASD. Early intervention provided by parents or professionals can help children to reach their potential. These children might be the next Temple Grandins of the world—brilliant visual thinkers who seek out their own strategies to cope with sensory defensiveness. These children might be the Carly Fleishmans—whose agitation, hyperactivity, and inability to communicate mask uniquely sweet and funny personalities. Given the right technology, they can blossom. These children might be like my own son, an extremely difficult to soothe baby who grew up to have exceptional fine motor skills. His executive functioning challenges still make academic and career success a long, slow, uphill battle. Nevertheless, my son has graduated from college with a degree in biology, is working on an engineering degree, and has backpacked half the Appalachian Trail, *solo!*

Finally, this book is written for all of the Garys out there. I can't help wondering what children like him could do if their parents used the strategies I described in this book. Would they be motivated to vary their play? Would they have better motor control? Would they tolerate touch better and possibly become artists? I hope that the answer is a resounding *yes!*

GLOSSARY

Applied Behavioral Analysis (ABA): An intervention that focuses on using positive reinforcements or rewards so that a desired behavior is likely to be repeated.

Ascender letters: Lowercase letters such as *h, l, f, t* and *b;* they sit on the base line but extend above the half-space letters such as *a, c, s,* or *i.*

Asperger's syndrome: A condition previously described as a type of higher functioning autism in the American Psychiatric Association's *Diagnostic and Statistical Manual,*4th edition (DSM-4). It is currently included in the fifth edition (DSM-5) as part of the autism spectrum.

Attention deficit/hyperactivity disorder (ADHD): A condition in which people show persistent inattention and/or hyperactivity-impulsivity that interferes with their functioning or development. Mental health professionals use specific behavior patterns to diagnose ADHD. These are listed in the DSM-5.

Auditory sense: One of the eight senses, the auditory sense perceives sound by detecting vibrations. This results in hearing.

Autism spectrum disorders (ASD): A neurobiological disorder. The DSM-5 lists diagnostic criteria in two areas: (1) weaknesses in social communication and social interactions across many contexts; and (2) restricted, repetitive patterns of behavior, interests, or activities.

Backward chaining: A teaching technique that breaks down multistep tasks (like zipping a jacket) into small steps. It involves teaching the child to learn and perform the last step(s) of a series first. Backward chaining may be most effective when the last steps are easier than earlier ones.

Base line (or **writing line**): On lined writing paper, the line that most letters sit on. Some letters, such as *g, j, p,* and *q,* dip below the base line.

Body awareness: An internal awareness that results from how a person's brain interprets and uses sensory information from touch and movement. Body awareness enables us to know where our body, arms, and legs are in space, and how our body parts are moving in relation to each other and the environment.

Brain hemispheres: The left and right sides of the brain.

Brain specialization: The location of specific abilities (such as language or visual perceptual discrimination) in one of the brain hemispheres. The term also refers to the development of dominance in one hemisphere (usually the left hemisphere) so that the person has greater skill on the opposite side (usually the right side).

Cause-and-effect relationship: The understanding that an action produces a result. For example, a baby learns that shaking a rattle produces a pleasant sound.

Cognitive abilities (or **skills**): The process of learning and using knowledge in order to solve problems. Cognitive skills enable us to carry out tasks such as counting or sorting objects by size.

Crossed (or **mixed**) **dominance:** The use of different hands for specific skills, or a hand and foot dominance that differ. Examples are using the right hand to write and left hand to grasp a spoon, or the right hand to throw a ball and left foot to kick one.

Crossing midline: Using the eyes or hands to look or reach past the imaginary line that runs down the center of the body (midline), dividing it into left and right sides.

Depth perception: The ability to use the eyes together to perceive three-dimensional objects. Depth perception enables us to judge the distance of an object and the relationships between objects such as keys and keyholes.

Descender letters: Letters with a portion that extends below the writing base line, such as *g, j, y, p,* or *q.*

Developmental optometrist (O.D.): A licensed vision care professional who diagnoses and treats visual health problems. Developmental optometrists specialize in evaluating how vision affects behavior and learning.

Diagnostic and Statistical Manual **(DSM):** A publication of the American Psychological Association that contains the standard classifications and diagnostic criteria of mental disorders recognized in the U.S. healthcare system. The 5th edition (referred to as DSM-5) was published in 2013.

Dyspraxia: one of six subtypes of **sensory processing disorders,** dyspraxia impacts abilities to plan and execute coordinated movements.

Executive functioning: Mental skills that enable a person to plan, organize, initiate, perform, and complete tasks.

Eye contact: A form of nonverbal communication. It occurs when two people look into each other's eyes at the same time.

Eye-hand coordination: The ability to use the eyes and hands together in a useful manner.

Eyesight: the ability to see or resolving power, as a result of light entering the eye.

Fine motor skills: Movements performed using small muscle groups, such as those in the hands.

Forward chaining: A method for teaching a sequence of steps by beginning with the first step and then adding the following steps once the first step is learned. Forward chaining may be most effective when the first step is easier than later ones (see also **backward chaining**).

Functional skills (or **life skills**): The everyday tasks people need to perform to be as independent as possible. They include hygiene, grooming, dining, and dressing skills.

Functional vision: The ability to use visual information to plan and perform tasks.

Generalization of skills: The ability to use a skill learned in one context or environment in a different situation. An example is to generalize using a spoon to scoop oatmeal from a bowl to scooping pudding out of a cup.

Gross motor skills: Movements performs using large muscle groups, such as the shoulders or legs.

Gustatory sense: One of the eight senses. The gustatory sensory receptors in the taste buds of the tongue enable us to taste.

Hand dominance: The result of **brain specialization** so that the hand opposite the dominant **brain hemisphere** develops greater skill.

Hand-over-hand assistance (HOH): A teaching technique in which the instructor places his/her hands over the child's hands. By guiding the child's hand movements the instructor helps the child experience what the motions feel like.

Hand preference: The consistent favoring of one hand to perform skilled tasks, such as writing. Although *hand preference* is sometimes referred to as **hand dominance,** the preferred hand is not necessarily opposite the dominant **brain hemisphere.**

Helper hand: The less skilled or non-preferred hand that is used to stabilize or support materials. Children can be taught that the **worker hand** (preferred or more skilled hand) controls a tool such as a pencil while the helper hand holds the paper steady.

Hippotherapy: The use of a horse as a treatment tool by a licensed OT, PT or SLP to work on therapeutic objectives as part of an intervention plan.

Hyper-reactivity (or **over-responsivity**): An atypically strong or exaggerated response to certain types of sensory stimulation. Children with hyper-reactivity may also be referred to as *hyper-responsive, super-sensitive,* or *sensory avoiders.*

Hypo-reactivity (or **under-responsivity**): An atypical or diminished response to certain types of sensory stimulation. Children with hypo-reactivity may also be referred to as *hypo-responsive* or *sensory seekers.*

Hypotonia: A neurological condition causing lower than normal tension, or resistance to stretch, in muscles. The person seems "floppy," "weak, " or "loose."

Interoception: One of the eight senses; it enables us to detect and respond to internal states such as hunger, heart rate, respiration, and elimination.

Isolated eye movements: Movements made with only the eyes while the head remains stationary.

Joint attention: A situation where two individuals share a focus on the same thing—often a person, object, or situation. It is achieved when one person alerts another to an object using verbal or nonverbal communication.

Learning disability (LD): A neurological difference in the way the brain is "wired" that affects how one learns. Different types of learning disabilities may create challenges with reading, writing, spelling, doing math, or organizing information.

Life skills: See **functional skills.**

Messy play: Activities using various substances, such as paint or sand, to develop awareness of touch (**tactile** sense) and motor skills.

Midline: An imaginary line that runs down the center of the body, dividing it into left and right halves.

Mixed dominance: See **crossed dominance.**

Motor planning (skills): The brain's organization of sensory information in order to plan and carry out new actions with ease and accuracy.

Muscle tone: The tension in muscles that enables us to maintain our posture. This tension determines how much resistance there is when our bodies move.

Multisensory: Used to describe an activity that stimulates two or more sensory systems. For example, a multisensory toy might make sounds, light up, and vibrate when squeezed.

Near senses: The tactile, proprioceptive and vestibular senses. They are called near senses because they are stimulated when the caregiver is in close contact with—holding or moving—the child. In contrast, senses such as vision, hearing, and smell can be stimulated from a distance.

Olfactory sense: One of the eight senses. The olfactory sensory receptors in the nose allow us to smell odors.

Orientation to writing line: The skill of placing letters or numbers with accuracy on the base or writing lines during the process of writing.

Peripheral vision: Use of the outer edges of the **visual field** as opposed to using a central, direct gaze. Peripheral vision is also described as *indirect*, *side*, or *eccentric* viewing.

Pervasive developmental disorder (PDD): A diagnostic umbrella term formerly listed in the DSM-4. It included 1) autism, 2) Asperger's syndrome, 3) pervasive developmental disorder, not otherwise specified, 4) Rett's disorder and 5) childhood disintegrative disorder. Now the DSM-5 describes autism as a broad spectrum ranging from low to high functioning.

Positive consequence: A desirable result that follows a behavior and increases the likelihood that the behavior will be repeated.

Postural control: The ability to reach or maintain stability and balance in a particular position such as sitting or during movement such as walking.

Postural disorder: One of six subtypes of **sensory processing disorders**. It involves difficulty maintaining adequate control of the body to meet the demands of a motor task. An example is sitting upright to work at a desk without leaning on one arm.

Prewriting skills: Abilities that are prerequisite to writing, such as grasping a writing tool and forming lines and circles.

Prone: The position of lying face-down (with chest down and back up).

Proprioceptive sense: One of the eight senses. Proprioceptive sensory receptors in the muscles, joints, and tendons interpret where the body and body parts are in space and how they are moving.

Quiet fidget tools: Commonplace, simple objects that we can fiddle with to calm ourselves or concentrate better. Examples are rolling a smooth rock between our fingers or squeezing a moldable eraser.

Reading guide: A strip with a small viewing area that is moved across a page or screen of text while reading. A reading guide can make reading easier or more comfortable.

Reinforcer: A consequence or result that occurs after a behavior that increases the likelihood that the behavior will be repeated. Reinforcers may also be called *rewards*. For example, a paycheck reinforces employees for coming to work.

Resistive activities: Tasks that require force to perform. They may involve pushing, pulling, or squeezing objects, or moving against our own body weight.

Scanning: The use of eye or head movements to search for and find an object(s) or detail(s) quickly and efficiently. We might scan a room to find a person, a table to find our keys, or a page to find a word.

Scotopic sensitivity (or **visual stress,** or **Irlen syndrome**): A disorder thought to create difficulty tolerating certain types of lighting. The word *scoptic* refers to vision under low light conditions.

Self-regulation: The ability to control our behavior, emotions, or thoughts and adapt to the demands of a situation.

Senses: People have the following eight senses that enable us to receive and respond to information from the environment and our bodies: (1) sight, (2) hearing, (3) taste, (4) smell, (5) touch, (6) vestibular, (7) proprioception, and (8) interoception.

Sensory-based motor disorders: A category encompassing **postural disorders** and **dyspraxia.** These are two of the six subtypes of **sensory processing disorders**.

Sensory craving: A term describing individuals who actively seek out and seem to have an insatiable appetite for sensory stimulation. Sensory craving is listed as one of the six subtypes of **sensory processing disorders**.

Sensory defensiveness: Atypical reactions or extreme sensitivities to sensory stimulation such as touch, sound, or movement.

Sensory diet: A collection of sensory-based activities or adaptations that help a child stay engaged and **self-regulated.** The sensory diet is individualized and carefully implemented to fit the needs of a specific child.

Sensory discrimination disorder: A subtype of **sensory processing disorders** that involves difficulties interpreting sensations.

Sensory fidget tools: Tools designed to meet the needs of children who seek and benefit from deep-pressure sensory stimulation to muscles and joints. These objects are often pulled, squeezed, or pushed.

Sensory modulation disorders: A category of **sensory processing disorders** that consists of (1) **sensory over-responsive,** (2) **sensory under-responsive,** and (3) **sensory craving.** Children with sensory modulation disorders have difficulties managing their responses to sensory stimulation in order to engage and learn.

Sensory-motor triad: The interactions of the vestibular, proprioceptive, and tactile senses to achieve **self-regulation** and coordination, and to perform everyday activities.

Sensory over-responsivity: See **hyper-reactivity.**

Sensory processing (SP) (or sensory integration): The process of taking in information from the environment through the sense organs; interpreting it in the brain; then using it in a functional way to move, play, and learn.

Sensory processing disorder (SPD): A condition that occurs when the brain has difficulty receiving, interpreting, and responding effectively to sensory information. There are six subtypes of SPD: (1) **sensory over-responsive,** (2) **sensory under-responsive,** (3) **sensory craving,** (4) **postural disorders,** (5) **dyspraxia,** and (6) **sensory discrimination disorder.**

Sensory reinforcer: A pleasant sensory experience that occurs after a specific behavior and that increases the likelihood of that behavior occurring again.

Sensory under-responsivity: See **hypo-reactivity.**

Stereotypical behaviors: Repetitive and/or restrictive movement or behaviors that are common in individuals with ASD. The DSM-5 includes restricted interests/repetitive behaviors as criteria for the autism diagnosis.

Success-only activities: Activities adapted so that they will only work when performed correctly. An example is a shape sorter where only the correct shapes fit through the corresponding openings.

Tactile: One of the eight senses. Tactile sensory receptors in the skin interpret and respond to both light and heavy touch sensations.

Tactile defensiveness: An unusually high sensitivity to touch sensations. It may cause a person to feel overwhelmed by or fearful of touch, or to refuse to touch certain textures.

Tactile discrimination: The ability to identify and differentiate information received through the sense of touch. The tactile system enables us to identify objects by touch and to recognize their shape, temperature, or texture.

Tripod pencil grasp: A pencil grasp that uses the middle finger, index finger, and thumb in a way that looks like a tripod stand. It is considered the most efficient pencil grasp for motor control and comfort.

Tummy time: A supervised activity where a baby is positioned face-down on the belly on top of a surface such as the floor, a parent's lap, or a bolster.

20/20 eyesight: Average or normal visual acuity or focusing power.

Vestibular sense: One of the eight senses. The vestibular sensory receptors are located inside the inner ears. They respond to the pull of gravity, changes in head movement and speed and play an important role in maintaining balance and developing motor skills.

Visual accommodation: The ability to keep objects in focus when moving our gaze between various distances and planes.

Visual field: The total area the eyes can see while gazing straight ahead. The visual field includes not only the area right in front of us, but also areas to the right and left, above and below.

Visual fixation: The coordination of our eyes to gaze at objects or people.

Visual perception: The brain's ability to make sense of the environment by using information received by the eyes. We use visual perception to match pictures or draw a picture. These are called *visual perceptual activities.*

Visual tracking: The ability to fixate on an object, then follow it while it is moving. An example is watching a bird in flight.

Visual sense: Vision is one of the eight senses. It involves using the eyes to process and respond to information contained in visible light.

Worker hand: The more skilled, usually dominant, hand that is used to perform complex tasks such as writing. (See also **helper hand**).

W-sitting: Sitting with both knees bent and legs turned outward away from the body, with feet outside the hips so that the legs are in the shape of the letter *W.*

Resources

● ● ●

Many of the products described in this section are sold through the following catalogs.

Educational/Therapy Catalogs or Websites

- Abilitations.com
- Autism-products.com
- Especialneeds.com
- Funandfunction.com
- Flaghouse.com/Sensory-Solutions
- Kidcompanions.com (sells chewable sensory products)
- Lakeshorelearning.com
- Nationalautismresources.com/sensory-integration.html
- Pfot.com
- RealOTsolutions.com
- Southpaw.com
- Specialneedstoys.com
- Therapro.com
- Therapyshoppe.com

ALL THINGS SENSORY

BOOKS AND WEBSITES FOR MORE INFORMATION

ALERT Program   **Alertprogram.com**
The ALERT Program is described in *How Does Your Engine Run*, by Sherry Shellenberger and Mary Sue Williams (1996), published and sold by Therapy Works.

All the Possibilities   **Allthepossibilitiesinc.com**
Occupational therapist Tere Bowen-Irish shares videos from her *Drive-Thru Menus* series. These demonstrate sensory based-activities designed to promote attention, strength, relaxation, and stress reduction.

Building Bridges through Sensory Integration
Book by Ellen Yack, Paula Aquilla, and Shirley Sutton (3rd edition, 2015), published by Sensory World (an imprint of Future Horizons). This book is a classic filled with many strategies.

GAIAM Life   **Life.gaiam.com**
See "How Sitting on a Ball Helps Kids Focus and Do Better in School: Bouncing Their Way to Better Grades!," by Karen Lynch, at **Life.gaiam.com/article/how-sitting-ball-helps-kids-focus-and-do-better-school**

Lucy Jane Miller Resources
Dr. Miller is the founder of the Sensory Processing Disorder Foundation.

STAR Institute for Sensory Processing Disorder **Spdstar.org/lucy-Lucy-miller-ph-d-otr**

YouTube video by Dr. Lucy Jane Miller
   www.youtube.com/watch?v=QDaj4daRWJc

No Longer a Secret
Book by Doreit Bialer and Lucy Jane Miller (2011), published by Sensory World (an imprint of Future Horizons).

Sensational Kids: Hope and Help for Children with Sensory Processing Disorder (SPD)
Book by Lucy Jane Miller (2014), published by TarcherPerigee (an imprint of Penguin USA).

Out-of-Sync-Child   **Out-of-sync-child.com**

The Out-of-Sync-Child
Book by Carol Kranowitz (revised edition, 2006), published by TarcherPerigee (an imprint of Penguin USA).

The Out-of-Sync Child Has Fun: Activities for Kids with Sensory Processing Disorder
Book by Carol Kranowitz (revised edition, 2006), published by TarcherPerigee (an imprint of Penguin USA).

Raising a Sensory Smart Child   **Sensorysmarts.com**

Raising a Sensory Smart Child
Book by Lindsey Biel and Nancy Peske (2009), published by Penguin Books.

Sensory Processing Disorder Foundation   **Spdfoundation.net**
A good source for general information.

SENSORY PRODUCTS
Vibration

- Children's motorized toothbrushes
- Hand-held massagers (sold in department stores and pharmacies)

- Hart Squiggle Wiggle Writer
- Jumping Joggle Bopper Vibrating Ball
- SENSEEZ® therapeutic cushions and pillows **Senseez.com**

Resistive Toys

- Tangle Toys sensory toys
- Stress balls
- Popping Martian or Bug Out Bob—when you squeeze hard the eyes pop out
- Toys with Velcro parts to pull off
- Building Bricks, Snap Cubes, K'nex or other construction toys that require force when pushed together

Oral Stimulation Materials

- Chewlry chewable jewelry (ARK Therapeutic Services, **Arktherapeutic.com/chewelry**)
- Chewables (Kid Companions, **Kidcompanions.com)**

Seating

- <u>Bungee chair</u>: sold in department stores
- <u>SENSEEZE vibrating pillows and cushions</u> **senseez.com**
- <u>Movin-Sit Air cushions:</u> These inflatable, wedge-shaped seat cushions come in small and large sizes.
- <u>Disc cushions and balance discs:</u> these inflatable, round disks have one bumpy side and one smooth side.

- <u>Ball chairs:</u> You can find several models in educational or thera-peutic catalogs. Some may have attached feet or a frame. You can place them inside a box to stabilize them or simply sit on them without additional support.

Weighted Products
These products are sold in most of the catalogs listed in this section.

- Vests
- Collars
- Blankets
- Lap bags
- Toys
- Gloves
- Wrist weights
- Compression, snug, or squeeze vests

ALL THINGS VISUAL AND VISUAL PERCEPTION

BOOKS AND WEBSITES FOR MORE INFORMATION
Developmental Optometry

<u>Age of Autism: Daily Web Newspaper of the Autism Epidemic</u>
ageofautism.com
See especially "Optometry's Role in Autism Spectrum Disorders," by Randy Schulman, MS, OD, FCOVD, **Ageofautism.com/2008/06/optometrys-role.html**

<u>College of Optometrists in Vision Development</u>   **COVD.org**
See especially "Autism and Vision," **Covd.org/?page=Autism**

Seeing through New Eyes
Changing the Lives of Children with Autism, Asperger Syndrome, and Other Developmental Disabilities through Vision Therapy, book by Melvin Kaplan (2005), published by Jessica Kingsley Publishers.

Developmental Delay Resources   **devdelay.org**
The DDR newsletter has an article by Melvin Kaplan, OD, "Behavior through a Lens" (**Devdelay.org/newsletter/articles/html/337-behavior-through-a-lens.html**)

VISION-RELATED ACTIVITIES OR ADAPTATIONS
Eye Can Learn Eye Exercises for Visual Health and School Success
Eyecanlearn.com

EyeGames: Easy and Fun Visual Exercises
By Lois Hickman and Rebecca Hutchins (2nd edition, 2010), published by Sensory World (an imprint of Future Horizons). A book of vision-enhancing exercises co-written by an OT and an optometrist.

Visual Techniques for Developing Social Skills
Activities and Lesson Plans for Teaching Children with High Functioning Autism and Asperger's Syndrome, book by Rebecca Moyes (2012) published by Future Horizons.

Visual Perception Problems in Children with AD/HD, Autism, and Other Learning Disabilities
A Guide for Parents and Professionals by Lisa A. Kurtz (2006), published by Jessica Kingsley Publishers.

Irlen® **irlen.com**
Find information about using the Irlen method for autism spectrum disorders at "Autism/Asperger Syndrome," **Irlen.com/autism-asperger-syndrome-the-irlen-method/**

Behavior and Executive Functioning

Books and Websites for More Information

No More Meltdowns
Book by Jed Baker (2008), published by Future Horizons. As the title suggests, the author shares strategies to prevent or minimize the occurrence of meltdown behaviors.

The Verbal Behavior Approach: How to Teach Children with Autism and Related Disorders
Book by Mary Barbera (2007), published by Jessica Kingsley Publishers. As a professional and a parent of a child with autism, the author shares her experiences using reinforcement to shape her son's behaviors.

Solutions for Parents and Families of Sensory Kids
Systemsforsensorykids.wordpress.com
A blog with tips for helping children with sensory issues get organized.

A Sensory Life   **Asensorylife.com**
For tips on understanding and reacting to meltdowns, see "Sensory Meltdowns. . .Par for the Sensory Course" at **Asensorylife.com/sensory-meltdowns.html.**

Indiana Resource Center for Autism   **iidc.indiana.edu**
See especially "Using Visual Schedules: A Guide for Parents" at **iidc.indiana.edu/pages/using-visual-schedules-a-guide-for-parents**

Visual Timers and Schedules

* Time Timer: This commercially available timer has a red section that enables children to visualize how much time is remaining, along with options for audible countdown.

- Learning Resources Time Tracker: The Time Tracker has programmed lights and sound cues to alert children how much time is remaining.
- Sand timers: You can find a variety of hourglasses and similar timers from many sources
- First Then Visual Schedule App: Developed by Good Karma Applications, available from ITunes at **itunes.apple.com/us/app/first-then-visual-schedule/id355527801?mt=8**

Hippotherapy and Animal-Assisted Therapies

American Hippotherapy Association (AHA)
Americanhippotherapyassociation.org
Learn how hippotherapy can help children with autism spectrum disorders.

Professional Association of Therapeutic Horsemanship International (PATH)   **Pathintl.org**
See "Learn About Therapeutic Riding" to find out how this therapy can help children with autism spectrum disorders **Pathintl.org/resources-education/faculty/27-resources/general/198-learn-about-therapeutic-riding.**

7 Senses Therapy   **7sensestherapy.com/#!tinder/c1atx**
Check out Tinder, the therapy dog at this clinic.

Animal-Assisted Interventions for Individuals with Autism
Book by Merope Pavlides (2008), published by Jessica Kingsley Publishers.

"What Is Hippotherapy?"   **Barbarasmithoccupationaltherapist. com/whatishippotherapy.html**

Handwriting

Books and Websites

Handwriting with Katherine   **Handwritingwithkatherine.com**
Occupational therapist Katherine Collmer shares many strategies for parents, teachers and therapists that teach foundational and handwriting skills.

I Hate to Write
Tips for Helping Students with Autism Spectrum and Related Disorders Increase Achievement, Meet Academic Standards, and Become Happy, Successful Writers, by Cheryl Boucher and Kathy Oehler (2013), published by AAPC Publishing.

Handwriting Without Tears, "Parents"   **Hwtears.com/hwt/parents**
The Handwriting without Tears books are written primarily for educators but this page shares tips for parents who use the books at home.

Parents Magazine Online   **parents.com**
Find videos that teach proper pencil grip and letter formation at **parents. com/videos/handwriting.htm.**

From Rattles to Writing: A Parent's Guide to Hand Skills
This book, written by me, Barbara Smith, (2011) and published by Therapro, Inc., describes how to help children develop the fine motor skills needed to write.

Handwriting Materials
Adapted fine motor and writing materials are sold in many of the listed catalog websites.

Paper

* <u>Raised line paper:</u> Tactile and visual cues indicate where to write.
* <u>Smart Start paper:</u> Color coded with a green ground line to write on, and a blue sky line for tall letters to reach.
* <u>Highlighter paper:</u> Indicates with color where to place letters.

Pencil Grips

* <u>Bulb-shaped grips</u>
* <u>Triangular-shaped grips</u>
* <u>Start-Right pencil grip:</u> A barrier prevents the thumb from crossing over the fingers.
* <u>Stetro grip:</u> A small grip with indentations for finger placement.
* <u>The Grip:</u> A larger grip with indentations for finger placement.
* <u>Bumpy grips:</u> Indentations guide finger placement and the bumpy texture prevents slippage.
* <u>Grotto grips:</u> A grip with a guard to maintain a tripod grasp.

Slant Boards

Slant boards vary in size, angle, and whether or not they are adjustable or collapsible. You can make your own out of a large book binder as described in this book in chapter 8.

Spacing Tools

* <u>One Finger Spacer:</u> A ruler with a single finger extended on top to create single spaces.
* <u>Two Finger Spacer:</u> A ruler with two fingers extended on top to create double spaces.

Scissors

- <u>Loop or squeeze-handled scissors:</u> These handles make it easier to coordinate opening and closing.
- <u>Self-opening scissors:</u> A spring is fitted to automatically reopen the blades once pressure is released.
- <u>Children's learning scissors:</u> Extra-small scissors for small hands are easier for young children to control.
- <u>Dual-control scissors:</u> Double loops on the handles allow an instructor to provide hand-over-hand guidance.

APPS FOR EDUCATION AND THERAPY

<u>Handwriting apps</u>   **Teachwithyouripad.wikispaces.com/ Handwriting+Apps**

<u>Apps that develop fine motor skills</u>   **A4cwsn.com/tag/fine motor**

<u>OT-recommended apps</u>   **Otswithapps.com/tag/fine motor-apps**

<u>Apps made by teachers</u>   **Fizzbrain.com**
Find apps to promote writing, eye contact, social skills, creative play, and rhythm and balance.

FUN CHILD DEVELOPMENT AND THERAPY WEBSITES AND BLOGS

- **BabyOT.com**
- **Candokiddo.com**
- **drannezachry.com/wordpress**
- **Growinghandsonkids.com**
- **HandwritingwithKatherine.com**

* MamaOT.com
* missawesomeness.com
* Missjaimeot.com
* Ot-mom-learning-activities.com
* Pinkoatmeal.com
* Playapy.com
* Proactivespeech.wordpress.com
* RecyclingOT.com
* Theinspiredtreehouse.com
* Thepocketot.blogspot.com
* TherapyFunZone.com
* Yourtherapysource.com
* Yourkidsot.com

Inspirational Sources about Autism Spectrum Disorders

Temple Grandin

* *Emergence: Labeled Autistic* (reissued edition, 1996), published by Warner Books
* *Thinking in Pictures: My Life with Autism* (revised edition, 2006), published by Vintage
* *The Way I See It, Revised and Expanded: A Personal Look at Autism and Asperger's* (2nd edition, 2011), published by Future Horizons.
* Templegrandin.com

Carly's Voice

* **Carlysvoice.com**
* *Carly's Voice: Breaking through Autism*, by Arthur Fleischmann with contributions by Carly Fleischmann (2012), published by Touchstone
* "Nonverbal Girl with Autism Speaks through Her Computer," a *20/20* story on Carly **Youtube.com/watch?v=xMBzJleeOno**

Stephen Shore

* **Autismasperger.net**
* *Beyond the Wall: Personal Experiences with Autism and Asperger Syndrome* (2nd edition, 2003), published by Autism Aspergers Publishing.

Do-It-Yourself Tips

• • •

WEIGHTED PRODUCTS

Consult with your occupational therapist to determine weight and wearing time.

How to make a weighted blanket
* A useful video is at **Youtube.com/watch?v=Qw_IzkB2Cz0**

How to make a weighted vest
I took an old fishing vest that had many pockets and filled them with sealed bags of sand.
Find instructions for making different types at

* **iamanautismparent.com/be-our-vest-be-our-vest-we-love-our-weighted-vests**
* **Littlemisskimberlyann.blogspot.com/2013/08/diy-weighted-sensory-vest-for-kids-with.html**

VISUAL AIDS

* "Best DIY Light Table Tutorials & Ideas" has instructions for building various kinds of light tables at **Wonderbaby.org/articles/best-diy-light-table-tutorials**
* "How to Make a Visual Schedule" YouTube video at **Youtube: Youtube.com/watch?v=SgEkHcipoy0**

CUTTING PLASTIC BOTTLES

Several activities in this book use large plastic detergent or dishwasher soap bottles. To cut these use heavy-duty leather shears or scissors sold in sewing or home stores. Cutting plastic will blunt them, so don't plan on using them for paper. Also you will need to replace or sharpen the blades regularly.

I initially jab the sharp tip into the bottle so that I can start cutting to create a general shape or flat pieces of plastic. Cut around a second time to make the edges smooth and even. I am often asked if these cut edges are sharp or dangerous. They feel rough but I can rub the plastic pieces across my face without getting cut. However, avoid making anything pointy that can poke the eyes.

Detergent bottles, especially the larger ones, are made of thick plastic that may be difficult to cut. Smaller detergent bottles and dishwasher soap bottles are generally made out of a softer, easier to cut plastic. So choose the bottle type according to the sturdiness of your scissors, your hand strength, and how sturdy the end product needs to be.

Punching holes through plastic: I purchased a hand-held heavy-duty hole-puncher from an office supply store for about $35.00. I use it to make lacing boards, arts and crafts projects, and the colorful little circles that can be used in shakers. The water bottle pegs shown in photo 13 are filled with these circles and tiny snippets of plastic.

WEDGING TUBES TO MAKE RING STACKS

Tubes may be cut from wooden dowels, PVC pipe, sturdy cardboard, or plastic dowel. Cut a hole in a box or bottle for the base. Be sure to cut the hole small enough that you have to push forcefully to wedge the tube in place. Then secure with duct tape. I often stuff the base with a bag of sand or fabric to hold the tube snugly in place. The ring stack shown in photo 11 was made by wedging part of a foam swimming noodle into a juice bottle. The noodle is a bit wobbly so that it takes two hands to use it—a good thing! In addition, I was easily able to push the vibrating device into the noodle opening to make it vibrate.

SANDBAGS

I typically make sandbags by filling a grocery bag partway with sand, tying a knot, then putting it in another bag to make it stronger. Tie another knot and repeat until you think that the bags won't leak. Squeeze out the air before you knot each bag or else the finished product will end up looking like a balloon. Sometimes I put the final bag inside a large sock or pillowcase that can be removed and washed as needed. Several of the activities described in this book use sandbags. Many children also enjoy just playing with sandbags, piling them up on their bodies or throwing them at a target.

NOTES

1. American Psychiatric Association, *Diagnostic and Statistical Manual of Mental Disorders*.4th ed. (Washington, DC: American Psychiatric Association, 1994).

2. American Psychiatric Association. *Diagnostic and Statistical Manual of Mental Disorders.* 5th ed. (Washington, DC: American Psychiatric Association; 2013).

3. SPD Foundation, *About SPD*, www.spdfoundation.net/about-sensory-processing-disorder/otherdisorders; Suzanne Allard Levingston, "The Debate over Sensory Processing Disorder: Are Some Kids Really 'Out of Sync'?" *Washington Post* online, washingtonpost.com/national/health-science/the-debate-over-sensory-processing-disorder-are-some-kids-really-out-of-sync/2014/05/12/fca2d338-d521-11e3-8a78-8fe50322a72c_story.html.

4. Heather Miller Kuhaneck, Susan L. Spitzer, and Elissa Miller, *Activity Analysis, Creativity and Playfulness in Pediatric Occupational Therapy: Making Play Just Right* (Burlington, MA: Jones & Bartlett Learning, 2010).

5. Ibid.

6. Temple Grandin and Margaret M. Scariano, *Emergence: Labeled Autistic* (Novato, CA: Arena Press, 1986).

7. Doreit S. Bialer and Lucy Jane Miller. *No Longer a Secret: Unique Common Sense Strategies for Children with Sensory or Motor Challenges* (Arlington, TX: Future Horizons, 2011).

8. Scott D. Tomchek and Jane Case-Smith, *Occupational Therapy Practice Guidelines for Children and Adolescents with Autism* (Bethesda, MD: AOTA Press, 2009).

9. Bialer and Miller, *No Longer a Secret.*

10. Jane Case-Smith, *Occupational Therapy for Children* (St. Louis, MO: Mosby, 2009).

11. A. Jean Ayres, *Sensory Integration and the Child* (Los Angeles: Western Psychological Services, 1979).

12. Anne H. Zachry, *Retro Baby: Cut Back on All the Gear and Boost Your Baby's Development with More Than 100 Time-Tested Activities* (Elk Grove Village, IL: American Academy of Pediatrics, 2014).

13. American Optometric Association, *Visual Acuity: What Is 20/20 Vision?* 2015, www.aoa.org/patients-and-public/eye-and-vision-problems/glossary-of-eye-and-vision-conditions/visual-acuity?sso=y.

14. Heather Miller Kuhaneck and Renee Watling, eds., *Autism: A Comprehensive Occupational Therapy Approach.* 3rd. ed. (Bethesda, MD: AOTA Press, 2010).

15. Heather Miller Kuhaneck, Susan L. Spitzer, and Elissa Miller, *Activity Analysis, Creativity, and Playfulness in Pediatric Occupational Therapy: Making Play Just Right* (Boston, MA: Jones & Bartlett Learning, 2009).

16. Randy Schulman, *Optometry's Role in Autism Spectrum Disorders*, 2008, www.ageofautism.com/2008/06/optometrys-role.html.

17. Lois Hickman and Rebecca E. Hutchins, *Eyegames: Easy and Fun Visual Exercises* (Arlington TX: Sensory World, 2011).

18. Jenifer Goodwin, "Babies May Show Signs of Autism," *USA Today*, August 9, 2010, http://usatoday30.usatoday.com/news/health/2010-08-09-autism-babies_N.htm.

19. "Managing Sensory Integration," *A Conversation on Autism*, 2016, www.aconversationonautism.com/Coping-with-Autism/Sensory-Integration

20. Temple Grandin, "Autism and Visual Thought," chapter 1 in *Thinking in Pictures*, available online at www.grandin.com/inc/visual.thinking.html.

21. Stephen M. Edelson, "Scotopic Sensitivity Syndrome and the Irlen Lens System," *Autism Research Institute*, www.autism.com/understanding_irlens.

22. "A Gift of Sight: Visual Perception Treatment for Autistic Children," *Your Health*, May 2016, http://chatham-kent.fitdv.com/new/articles/article.php?artid=1108.

23. Kuhaneck and Watling, *Autism*.

24. Peg Dawson and Richard Guare, *Executive Skills in Children and Adolescents*, 2nd ed. (New York: Guilford Press, 2010).

25. Ayres, *Sensory Integration and the Child*.

26. Case-Smith, *Occupational Therapy for Children*.

27. Mary Sue Williams and Sherry Shellenberger, *How Does Your Engine Run?* (Albuquerque, NM: Therapy Works, 1996).

28. *The ALERT Program*, www.alertprogram.com.

29. Jed Baker, *No More Meltdowns* (Arlington TX: Sensory World, 2008).

30. Arthur Fleishmann, *Carly's Voice: Breaking through Autism* (New York: Simon & Schuster, 2012).

31. Lois Jean Brady, *Apps for Autism* (Arlington, *TX:* Future Horizons, 2015).

32. Doapp, Inc., *The Farm Animals*, available at https://itunes.apple.com/us/app/farm-animals/id321061962?mt=8.

33. Claireware Software, *I Hear Ewe*, available at https://itunes.apple.com/us/app/i-hear-ewe-animal-sounds-for/id304093970?mt=8

34. Joe Scrivens, *Balloon Pops*, available at https://itunes.apple.com/us/app/balloon-pops/id436692552?mt=8.

35. AppVenturous, *Falling Apples*, available at https://itunes.apple.com/us/app/falling-apples-free/id369114527?mt=8.

36. Learning Touch, *First Words Sampler*, available at https://itunes.apple.com/us/app/first-words-sampler/id312571156?mt=8.

37. ngmoco, *MazeFinger Plus*, available at www.148apps.com/app/293559498/.

38. Binary Labs, *Dexteria*, available at www.dexteria.net/.

39. Sanoma, *Letter School*, available at www.letterschool.com/

40. Essare, *Ready to Print*, available at http://apps.essare.net/app/ready-to-print/.

41. Cheryl Boucher and Kathy Oehler, K., *I Hate to Write!* (Lenexa, KS: AAPC, 2013).

42. Sybil M. Berkey, *Teaching the Moving Child* (Baltimore, MD: Brookes, 2009).

About the Author

● ● ●

Barbara A. Smith, MS, OTR/L started out in human services as a live-in residential counselor for nine developmentally disabled men who moved from a large institution into a true home in an upstate New York community. After discovering she had a talent for helping people to be as independent as possible, Barbara earned her master's degree from Tufts University's Boston School of Occupational Therapy in 1984. In addition, she has earned certifications in sensory integration and hippotherapy.

Barbara has worked for more than 30 years in settings that include public schools, early intervention programs, community residences, state schools, and hippotherapy farms. She is the author of *The Recycling Occupational Therapist; The Almost Complete Plastic Bottle Activity Book; Still Giving Kisses: A Guide to Helping and Enjoying the Alzheimer's Victim You Love;* and *From Rattles to Writing: A Parent's Guide to Hand Skills.* Barbara has also published extensively in trade and parenting magazines and is a nationally recognized speaker and creator of online continuing education courses. Please visit **RecyclingOT.com** for more information.

Barbara currently lives in Massachusetts with her husband. In her spare time she enjoys hiking, roller-skating, and reading literature.

Other books by Barbara A. Smith

● ● ●

The Recycling Occupational Therapist

Still Giving Kisses: A Guide to Enjoying and Helping the
Alzheimer's Victim You Love

The Almost Complete Plastic Bottle Activity Book

From Rattles to Writing: A Parent's Guide to Hand Skills

As an occupational therapist who specializes in handwriting assessment and remediation, I find *From Rattles to Writing* to be one of my "go-to" resources for parent information, skill development ideas, and research information for my own writing. Barbara guides you through the developmental stages with pictures; clearly written explanations about the purpose of each activity; and easy, inexpensive, crafty ideas for facilitating a child's development. Occupational therapy terms can be confusing; but Barbara shares them with the reader with a clear idea of her diverse audience—using laymen's terms and pictures to clarify. I enjoy her writing style and encourage new parents to grab hold of this book and run with it! Your child will thank you for it!

—Katherine J. Collmer, MEd, OTR/L, Author of *Handwriting Development Assessment and Remediation*, **HandwritingwithKatherine.com**

● ● ●

Barbara worked with my two-year-old premature twins . . . (her) talented approach was simultaneously challenging and fun . . . a wonderful asset to my kids' progress. It is exciting to see her share her many creative ideas with other parents.

—Denise R. Sargent, PT, MS, physical therapy instructor